FAITH ALWAYS WORKS
The Death of a Believer

David Meseg

To my faithful wife Krissie
From your very blessed husband
David

Grosvenor House
Publishing Limited

This book is published by
Grosvenor House Publishing Ltd
Link House
140 The Broadway, Tolworth, Surrey, KT6 7HT.
www.grosvenorhousepublishing.co.uk

A CIP record for this book
is available from the British Library

ISBN 978-1-83975-661-0

Faith Always Works

The Death of a Believer

I dedicate my writing to my precious family: Krissie, Lucy and James, a family who has meant so much to me, more than they could possibly know. For you, my heart's burning desire is that you know and trust Jesus to be both your Saviour and Lord. It is only through Him that we will be reunited in God's gracious eternal kingdom. At the very least, I pray that my writing will serve as a lasting legacy to you, as it continues to speak into your lives long after I am gone.

'Behold! I tell you a mystery. We shall not all sleep, but we shall all be changed in a moment, in the twinkling of an eye, at the last trumpet. For the trumpet will sound, and the dead will be raised imperishable, and we shall be changed. For this perishable body must put on the imperishable, and this mortal body must put on immortality. When the perishable puts on the imperishable, and the mortal puts on immortality, then shall come to pass the saying that is written:

Death is swallowed up in victory.
O death, where is your victory?
O death, where is your sting?

The sting of death is sin, and the power of sin is the law. But thanks be to God, who gives us the victory through our Lord Jesus Christ. Therefore, my beloved brothers, be steadfast, immovable, always abounding in the work of the Lord, knowing that in the Lord your labour is not in vain.'

(1 Cor. 15:50–58)

Contents

PART THREE:
FAITH, MINISTRY AND HEALING

Foreword

Why write? I don't know; I just started to write on impulse. I am 56 years old, and the date today is 27 October 2016. I have decided to write since I do not know if I will have the ability or opportunity to do so later. As I write, I am an inpatient at the Royal Marsden in Chelsea, London. I am here to begin a new drug treatment for my cancer, and the consultants have said that the average life expectancy for someone who starts this treatment is about eight months. So, the clock is ticking. That clock is not just ticking for me; it is ticking for you also.

All of us are at risk of death the moment we leave the safety of our mother's womb. Whatever precautions we might take to keep ourselves safe, we can do nothing to stop the ticking of our biological clock. Different parts of the body begin to lose their battle against time at different ages as the cells in our bodies are destined to deteriorate and decline. For example: the brain (which starts with around 100 billion nerve cells or neurons), lungs and skin begin to age in our 20s, bones, muscle, hair, breasts and fertility in our 30s, heart and eyes in our 40s, gut, kidneys, prostate and hearing in our 50s, taste, smell, voice, in our 60s, liver and bladder in our 70s. If you have got this far, you have probably done so with the aid of medication or surgery.

I have learnt that there is only one way to approach life and that is to take it one precious day at a time. That is how we should all be living. No matter how healthy or wealthy we may be, none of us has the right to tomorrow which may never come. This approach provides me with a sense of urgency, together with an appreciation for each new day. Taking just one day at a time prevents me from living with a dangerous, casual approach to both life and death.

The question is, are any of us prepared for today to be our last day? Are we ready for what follows after our last breath? What if death brought us into the biggest surprise of our life? What if we did not find ourselves in a state of nothingness, but in a state of deep regret and extreme shock? What if we expected to be ushered into heaven, only to find out that, while heaven does exist, we do not qualify to be there?

What if we found out that the way we live our life is going to have a profound effect on our eternal destiny? Whether we agree with it or not, the Bible warns us of the coming Day of God's Judgment, when He will pass sentence on every person who has ever lived.

The context of my writing comes from within the messiness and pain of life that allows me to examine whether faith is real and does something, or whether it holds no meaningful purpose.

If faith is not real and does not work, then Christianity does not work and is nothing more than a religious hoax invented by unscrupulous men, who have created a money-making institution to gain some kind of power and influence over gullible people. However, what if faith is real and does do something? What does that something actually do?

Krissie has asked on numerous occasions who I am aiming my book at. Let me say that I have not set out to write a book for a larger audience, but if it finds itself in that arena, so be it. All I can say is that I am not an academic or an intellectual, which means that this 'book' is not likely to satisfy the demands of an academic or intellectual audience. I am an ordinary, simple person, so I suppose my writing is aimed at the ordinary person who is willing to read it. Nevertheless, I hope my writing has something to say to everyone, since the validity of faith is something that concerns each one of us, regardless of who we are. My writing is not a theological exposition on the matter of faith, neither is it sourced from various theological textbooks. Instead, it is freely written and expressed from my own personal experience as I seek to connect a real faith in a real God to the reality of real life and real death. My examination and understanding of what a real faith is was predominantly formed while I was in what I call my Desert Place. This was a place of tremendous despair as well as a place of tremendous spiritual revelation and insight, a place I shall reveal a little later on.

I do not profess for one moment to have everything mapped out or figured out, and I would caution you to stay well clear of anyone who claims that they do. I have been a Christian for many years, and I am still learning how to live out a real faith in a real world and will continue to do so till the day I die. In this book, I have expressed my views, something we all have, but my opinion does not really count for much. I do not write in a bid to be patted on the back, win the approval of others, or make people happy or angry. The only approval I seek is God's, and the authority I stand under is the authority of God's word as written in the Bible.

I hope that in this book, I have adequately made the point that the book we must all go to is the Bible. That ancient book is not man's word to us but God's word to us. If you think that faith in God is a waste of time and energy, you will also write off the Bible. But, for obvious reasons, the Bible has to be my starting point and point of reference since the Bible is how God has primarily chosen to reveal Himself to us. In it, God does not express His opinion, but tells us the truth about both Himself and ourselves. Throughout the pages of the Bible, God does not seek our approval or expect us to change or adapt His word to suit our own ends. My book takes the position that the Bible is God's inspired word to us, whatever the science, culture, time or place.

With that in mind, I write a book that seeks to take an honest look at how faith connects to real life. Sometimes it is very hard to have faith in a God who seems to be so far removed from our everyday experiences, especially when things go wrong. Those are the times when faith doesn't appear to work because God seems to be so distant, so unhelpful, uncaring and so unreal. Yet I have learnt that it is *especially* in the tough times that faith has the potential and power to become so real, valid and proving its worth. Anyone who claims to have a faith needs to understand what faith is and what it isn't, what it does and what it leads to. I hope this book will both encourage and challenge anyone who takes the time to read it.

Too many Christians today have a nominal faith, a faith that has a very poor understanding of what faith actually is. They have a belief in Jesus, yet that belief does not result in a life that is any different from the good, decent person who is an atheist or an agnostic. I would say that to have a nominal faith is more dangerous than having no faith, for when life does not go according to plan and our superficial faith makes no difference, the result is a disillusioned Christian who concludes that both faith and prayer do not work. More often than not, God gets all the blame or is written off entirely.

A correct understanding of faith paves the way for incredible hope, security and joy. At its core, faith stands in awe of the Almighty God and trusts in Jesus as Saviour, whether times are good or bad. True faith sees who God is and what He has accomplished, especially for those whose heart's desire is to belong to Him. True faith sees the love and grace of God demonstrated so powerfully at the cross of Jesus. At the cross, there is a plentiful supply of fuel to fill our hearts and minds with such a glorious appreciation of Jesus for the rest of our earthly lives. Such appreciation stems from a faith that makes all the difference, both in life and death.

Faith Always Works

The Death of a Believer

§

Part One

WHY FAITH?

Chapter 1

THE TRUTH ABOUT SIN

We cannot have a correct understanding of what faith is or what it does unless we have a correct understanding of what sin is, what it does and how offensive it is to God. This is crucial to our understanding of salvation and what salvation is.

The older we become and the more experience we gain about how this world ticks, the more we recognize that the world is ablaze with so many things we don't like. We hate war, crime, injustice and the abundance of so much evil and wickedness. We are offended by the aggression and dishonesty of others who tell blatant lies and try to get away with whatever they can. We recognize that the world is full of lies, selfishness and evil, and that very few people can be trusted to tell the honest truth about anything. This being said, we are more prone to recognize the shortcomings in other people than we do in ourselves.

Jesus said that the father of lies is the Devil, who does not hold to the truth because there is no truth in Him (John 8:44). At the very beginning of creation, in the purity and perfection of the Garden of Eden, the Devil (sometimes called the serpent, Satan) deceived the very first human beings that God created, Adam and Eve. The lie was that they could become like God. Adam and Eve were seduced by the Devil's temptation and disobeyed God's command not to eat the fruit from the tree of knowledge of good and evil. As a result, the curse of God fell upon the whole earth and especially upon Adam and Eve, who were the representatives of the whole human race. Even to this day, the father of lies continues to sow his deception throughout the world, deceiving the many into believing that they can be their own god.

Today, especially in the West where history has been shaped by Christianity and its ethics, we see this lie working its way out into the cultural and secular way of thinking. Such thinking, which is deemed to be progressive and pragmatic, says that one can believe in anything, everything or nothing. The moral absolutes of the Christian past are being eroded very fast to pave the way for a culture that says truth is relative and can be whatever you want it to be. In the process, culture 'de-gods' God by insisting that the culture of the day has the right to determine what is right and what is wrong, what is acceptable and what is not, what is evil and what is good. Some hold to the opinion that so long as others are not going to be hurt, you can do what you like.

Others, who prefer to live a less secularized, materialistic life, go in search of something spiritual. One only needs to browse through the Spirituality and Religion sections of a high street bookstore to gain a perspective on what is on offer for those who are seeking for a spiritual meaning to their lives. There are books galore that tell you there are many different ways to find God. They say that there is nothing to fear in life, it is just a matter of tuning in to the spiritual energy of the god within you that will release peace and happiness. Death, they say, is just another adventure, a voyage of discovery that paves the way for the spiritual realm, whatever that may be. Yet others hold to the existence of a divine, supernatural being that is the essence of love. They say that there is a God of some sort and that this God *needs* you and *wants* you; you simply need to recognize and accept His unconditional love for you. Other belief systems such as the Mormons, Jehovah Witnesses, Islam and Roman Catholicism offer a spirituality that has deviated from the Old and New Testament teachings of the Bible. These teachings have been added to or had things taken away, giving rise to cultic beliefs. Other belief systems such as Buddhism, Hinduism and the New Age movement are driven by some form of spiritualism and mysticism. Some of these claim that their system involves no belief at all but is entirely based on an inner knowing that comes from within a deep inner realization that awakens one's true, higher self.

All of these belief systems hold to what they believe to be the truth about life, death and the spiritual realm. Interestingly, quite a few of them have their own version of Jesus, yet he is not the Jesus of the Bible but a twisted, distorted version. I am not writing to discuss other religions or belief systems, but I am writing to say that what *kind* of Jesus a person believes in is hugely significant. At stake here is knowing what is true and what is false and therefore a lie.

Surely all religions and spirituality lead to the same God, regardless of the methods and words used to approach and describe Him (or her, or it)? At this point, I need to explain why I believe in the God of the Bible and why I believe He is the *only* one true God. Put simply, I believe in the God of the Bible because I believe in the Jesus of the Bible. Shortly before His crucifixion, Jesus prayed to God His Father in heaven for His followers:

> *'Father, the hour has come; glorify your Son that the Son may glorify you, since you have given him authority over all flesh, to give eternal life to all whom you have given him. And this is eternal life that they know you, the only true God, and Jesus Christ whom you have sent. I glorified you on earth, having accomplished the work that you gave me to do. And now, Father, glorify me in your own presence with the glory that I had with you before the world existed'* (John 17:1–5).

From this passage alone (and there are many more), we can see that Jesus came *from* God, was sent *by* God, and that the God He prayed to was the only one true God. The Bible teaches us that after the crucifixion, death and burial of Jesus, God vindicated this same Jesus by raising Him back to life, who then appeared to hundreds of His followers before ascending back into heaven. Now if Jesus rose from the dead, I had better take Him seriously and pay close attention to what He did and everything that He said. His resurrection from the dead qualifies His right to be taken very seriously.

Jesus said of Himself:

> *'I am the way and the truth and the life. No one comes to the Father except through me'* (John 14:6).

> *'For this purpose, I was born and for this purpose I have come into the world—to bear witness to the truth. Everyone who is of the truth listens to my voice'* (John 18:37).

When the Apostle Peter was placed under interrogation by the Jewish authorities, he boldly proclaimed:

> *'And there is salvation in no one else, for there is no other name under heaven given among men by which we must be saved'* (Acts 4:12).

The Apostle John, one of Jesus's 12 disciples, writes:

> *'For God did not send his Son into the world to condemn the world, but in order that the world might be saved through him'* (John 3:17).

What did Jesus come to save the world from? He came to save the world from sin. How was Jesus to do that? Luke records the words of Jesus and writes:

> *'Those who are well have no need of a physician, but those who are sick. I have not come to call the righteous, but sinners to repentance'* (Luke 5:31–32).

The Bible teaches that every human being is born spiritually sick and unrighteous before God. The biblical way of looking at this is to recognize that every human being suffers from the spiritual disease of sin, and that Jesus came to save and heal the sinner from the disease of sin. If we want to understand what biblical faith is, we first need to have a proper understanding of what sin is, together with its consequences. A correct understanding of sin leads to a healthy fear of God and an understanding that a person's greatest ever need in this life is to be released from the guilt of their sin and get right with God. A lot of religious people today have very little fear of God and have changed Him into a God who, if you press all the right buttons, is okay with sin and loves all sinners unconditionally. In this way, sin has been trivialized and normalized, and we become desensitized to its offensiveness against a Holy God.

The Presence of Sin

I have acquired a deep hatred of sin, especially in this last year (2016). The presence of sin is everywhere, and all of us can testify to its destructive, divisive, seductive manifestations. I have stayed in hospitals watching other cancer victims battle for their lives. I look at the man in the bed opposite me right now, fighting his own war against cancer. All of this is a consequence of the presence of sin. I hate sin. I see the presence of sin all around me, in our attitude towards one another: jealousy, murder, hatred, crime, violence, dishonesty, disrespect, deception, sexual immorality, adultery and so much more. I see the presence of sin in individuals: envy, greed, selfishness, lust, disobedience, rebellion and pride. I see the manifestation of sin in the abuse of power, authority, money and sex. I see the abuse that leads to poverty and hunger. I see the evil of sin in the horrors of war and acts of terror that inflict so much insanity, brutality and bloodshed. I hate sin. I hate all the heartache, pain, sorrow, injustice and misery that it gives birth to.

I hate sin. Hate is a strong word but there is nothing nice or lovely to say about sin. Sin is inherently evil and destructive. Sometimes I find myself weeping because it grieves me so much. I loathe it, and it makes me angry because something so terrifyingly huge is not right with this world. This is not how it was meant to be. God created an astonishingly beautiful, perfect world, and I hate to see how sin has ruined that perfection. I hate to see how sin has ruined the perfect people that God created us to be. The world of today is a broken world full of broken people. Sin disfigures the perfection of health, which is why so many people of all ages suffer such cruelty inflicted upon their bodies and minds. Worst of all, sin has destroyed the perfect relationship that God originally created us to enjoy with Him. Sin is what separates and alienates us from a Holy God. It is the reason we cannot see Him with our eyes or hear Him with our ears. Sin pollutes and is best described as darkness. On the other hand, God is pure and full of light. If He were to appear before us now in all of His glory and splendour, none of us would be able to stand before Him and survive. In God there is no sin. God is gloriously Holy because of His purity, perfection, character and nature. There is no higher glory than that of God because He is total and complete in all goodness. There is no place for sin in His glorious presence, which is why we are so far removed and alienated from Him. I hate the presence of sin and its immense power to hold and enslave. Sin is like a drug; very powerful, seductive, addictive and full of deception. Sin fulfils our carnal desires and disguises itself in so many different ways. In this way we love sin and delight in it. In one form or another, it supplies us with pleasure, satisfaction and excitement. The problem is, because we do not recognize the glory of God, we do not recognize ourselves as sinners. We are blinded by our own sin because we are spiritually dead to God.

Sin is ugly and vile. It is no respecter of person. Sin is to be found in both good and bad people, the respectable and the villain. Babies and very young children have a beauty about them because they seem to be so innocent and free from evil. They have not yet learnt the difference between right and wrong, good or bad. As they grow up from childhood, they develop a conscience and begin to learn the difference between right and wrong. From then on, they get to choose between right and wrong, good and evil. This is when the presence of sin becomes evident. Have you ever noticed how a child does not need to be taught how to be selfish or to lie and disobey? Those things are inbuilt and ingrained into our corrupted human nature. Most of us would like to think that once we slip into adulthood, our conscience guides us to make the right choices and live life doing what is good and right. Others, however, seem to enjoy and thrive on doing wrong rather than right, displaying a conscience that has been seared or suppressed.

The Bible teaches that even the good we do is sin (Isaiah 64:6). You might think that I have lost the plot by making that last statement, but if you do, you reveal that you do not understand what sin is. Sin is to crave other things more than God. Sin craves to live for our own glory and our own reputation. Sin places me in the number one spot, and life is all about me and what makes me feel good. Our sinful acts and cravings simply flow from our sinful condition. It is a reflection of who we are at the core. No matter how nice, decent and perfect we may be, we perpetually live in this condition of sin. It is a condition that has removed God from His rightful position, which is to be at the very centre of our lives. The deception of sin leads to a life that lives independently of God, going our own way instead of His way. Therefore, even the good that we do, if it is done independently of God, is a continuation of living a sinful life. If this is the case, none of us, including myself, are capable of getting through any one day without sinning against God. I hate the presence of sin that I still see in myself, in what I say, think, do and do not do. I hate sin because it is so opposed to God. Sin is why our bodies die. Sin is the reason I have cancer. My cancer is a powerful daily reminder that I live in a broken body and a broken world. As hard as I try, I am powerless to bring myself into a sinless state or heal myself. The power of sin and its consequences are too powerful for any human to overcome or master.

No One is Perfect

In the eyes of Holy God, none of us are good because, through Adam, all of us have lost our state of innocence. While I may have my rare moments of what seem to be perfect moments, I know that I am incapable of living every moment for God's glory. The truth is, even on my best days, and no matter how hard I try not to be, I am imperfect in the eyes of a perfect God. The only way I can be made perfect is for Jesus Christ to give me His perfection.

The Sting of Sin is Death

Like sin, death is no respecter of person. We are all sinners, which is why we all die. The Bible tells us that; *'the sting of sin is death'* (1 Cor. 15:56). Elsewhere it tells us:

> *'For the wages of sin is death, but the free gift of God is eternal life in Christ Jesus our Lord'* (Rom. 6:23).

I am confident that everyone agrees that at some point in time, all of us will die. What we might not agree on is what happens after the death of our bodies. The Bible teaches us that our bodily death is not the end of our story:

> *'And just as it is appointed for man to die once, and after that comes judgment, so Christ, having been offered once to bear the sin of many, will appear a second time, not to deal with sin but to save those who are eagerly waiting for him'* (Heb. 9:27–28).

That judgment will come as a shock to the vast majority of people.

Life is Fragile

We only have to listen to the news to be reminded on a daily basis just how fragile life is.

We assume certain things will take place on any given day because they always do. We assume certain things will not

8

happen because they never do. We go through the day basing our expectations on these assumptions.

Nevertheless, the unexpected does and will happen. When those times hit, we can no longer deny the reality of death, and our eyes are opened to see how very fragile and unpredictable life is. We are brought home to the reality that there are so many things in our day that are outside of our control. Many of us live in fear of losing what we have made of our lives, those things that make us feel happy, wealthy and healthy: our family, marriage, home, career, friends, looks and so on. In today's world of social media, we advertise and promote our happiness by broadcasting it for the world to see. We want the world to know what happy people we are and what exciting, enjoyable lives we live. Such pretence presents a false facade that deceives the world into thinking that we are much happier than we actually are.

What scares us the most is the reality that something most unwelcome might be inflicted upon us without a moment's notice. We live in denial of this reality by accepting that these things are more likely to happen to other people and not us. We shrug off this reality by fostering a blasé attitude of whatever will be will be, or that everything happens for a reason (presumably a good reason). Some of us hide away from reality by thinking only positive thoughts. We stay clear of people who we know are going through a tough time for fear they might upset our positive mindset. We adopt various forms of escapism to protect ourselves from reality. A lot of people attempt to escape the mundane reality of their own lives and fears by entering into the lives of other people and into another world of make-believe through reading books and watching TV.

We Only Have One Life

Understandably, we only plan for our good and happiness so that we can get the best out of our day and our lives. Our goal is to be content, to be liked and successful. However, deep down we all have to live with the knowledge that nothing about today is certain. There are no guarantees that our day or life will turn out as we would like or expect. Reality tells us that we must always be prepared to face the unexpected, things we did not plan or hope for. Some desperate people wake up to the day feeling that happiness is something beyond their grasp. Their life has become a matter of survival, living from one day to the next in what seems to be a meaningless existence. Tragically, some decide to take the uncertainty out of life by choosing to end their own lives. Others wake to the same day full of hope and expectation but are not aware that they are waking up to their very last day; before the day is spent, their life is unexpectedly taken away from them by someone else or through some fatal accident or natural disaster.

We All Die but Try Hard Not To

Every day, we are reminded that we all die sooner or later. These reminders are sent our way whenever we stumble across a passing hearse or pass by a graveyard. The news media relentlessly remind us of death, all of which should serve to wake us up and remind us of our own frailty and vulnerability. We shrug it all off by consoling ourselves that it was someone else and not us. We have become so desensitized to the reality of death, especially since we see so much of it in the movies. The media entertains us with murder, disaster and death. Yet through it all, we know that none of us can escape our own death. How ever it comes, we will not find our own death entertaining.

The biggest fear most of us have may not be death itself but the dying process that takes us there. Nevertheless, virtually everyone fears death itself because of its finality. We certainly do not welcome death unless it releases us from unbearable pain and misery. In the normal scheme of things, death is seen as an inconvenience which spoils our fun, and so we try our best to avoid the whole issue by ignoring it as much as we can. Nonetheless, the Bible teaches us that while the death of our bodies brings an end to our physical life, it is not the end of us as

10

a person (Heb. 9:27). God created each one of us with a body and soul. The soul lies at the core of who we really are, and in this sense, you are a soul that has a body. Having a soul and body is what makes us fully human. The soul does not cease to exist at the point of physical death. The death of the body is not the real problem; it is simply the symptom of what the real problem is. The real problem is that the spirit (which is interchangeable with the word soul) is dead to God and separated from Him. Many people spend their whole lives taking great care over the condition of their physical bodies but pay no attention to the condition of their souls, since they do not believe they have one. While such people might fear the process of dying, they presume that once the end has come, there is nothing left to fear since there is nothing left of them. The Bible teaches something altogether different and that after death comes the Judgment. Many may fear death, yet they do not fear the judgment of God which follows the death of the body. God cannot judge a dead body, but He can judge the soul. The judgment of God is to be feared far more than the death of the body itself. Jesus gave this warning:

> '*I tell you my friends, do not fear those who kill the body, and after that have nothing more that they can do. But I will warn you whom to fear: fear him who, after he has killed, has authority to cast into hell. Yes, I tell you, fear him!*' (Luke 12:4–5).

> '*And do not fear those who kill the body but cannot kill the soul. Rather fear him who can destroy both soul and body in hell*' (Matt. 10:28).

In these passages, the one whom Jesus warns us to fear is God Himself. For the one who belongs to Jesus, death is not to be feared since it is the doorway into heaven, but for those who do not belong to Jesus, death is to be feared because it is the doorway into hell.

A lot of people in the Christianized West who possess a superficial faith, have either never had a healthy fear of God or have jettisoned it because they have been told that the God to be feared belongs to the Old Testament, whereas the God of the New Testament is love. They say that because they have faith in a good, loving God, there is no need to fear Him. They believe that this very loving God will consider them good enough for heaven because they go to church once a week. I dare say that many people believe they are good enough for heaven simply because they have not behaved like Adolf Hitler and that their good deeds far outweigh their bad deeds. Together with those who have no faith, a lot of people are going to get the shock of their lives when they find out that the death of the physical body is not the end, and that heaven *does* exist, but they are not good enough to go there.

Perhaps you have no faith and you have made up your mind to sleep in the bed you have made. Perhaps you have no faith and plan to think about these things nearer the time of your death. The thing is, you cannot afford the luxury of assuming that such an opportunity will come your way. Your life may be taken away tonight by a sudden, unexpected event and then it will be too late. I hope that this book will get all who read it to think more deeply about the reality of the desperate situation in which they find themselves. The truth is that everything between our birth and death is full of uncertainty. A lot of people do not allow themselves to think too deeply about these things because it leaves them feeling insecure and gloomy. Because of the reality of death, a sensible person cries out for an explanation for its existence. A mindset that refuses to think too deeply about life and death leaves no room for thinking about God, and in the shallowness of our thinking, we block God out. Instead, we distract ourselves by everything that the world has to offer us in the here and now. We only think about God if we are free to make up our own version of a God who suits our own way of life and beliefs. The serious flaw in this approach is that such a God cannot save anyone from their sinful condition and death.

Chapter 2

THE ABSENCE OF GOD

What Has Gone Wrong?

On the sixth day of creation, God created Adam.

'So God created man in his own image, in the image of God he created him; male and female he created them' (Gen.1:27).

In Genesis 2:7 we read:

'...then the LORD God formed the man of dust from the ground and breathed into his nostrils the breath of life, and the man became a living creature.'

God created the physical body of Adam, into which He breathed the breath of life. In this way, Adam became a living soul and, together with Eve, who was created from out of Adam, became the pinnacle of all that God had created. It was the 'soul' aspect that separated them from everything else that God had created, equipping them to enjoy living in direct communion with God. All of mankind that has flowed from the union of Adam and Eve, including you and me, have inherited the same body and soul composition. While I can see, touch and feel my body, the same cannot be said about my soul because it is not part of the physical realm. The soul is the primary substance of my immaterial existence, forming the essence of who I really am. There is a close, inseparable correlation between the soul and spirit. Since God is Spirit (John 4:24), I can only commune with Him in my spirit.

13

The fact we cannot see or touch our soul creates a problem for people who do not believe in the spiritual realm. They only believe in what they can see, which is why they refuse to believe in God. Surgeons can only deal with our physical bodies, since they can find no evidence of our spirit when they open up our bodies. Indeed, what proof or evidence is there that the spiritual realm even exists? For that matter, how am I expected to have faith in a God who I cannot see with my eyes?

I do not need faith to see what a beautiful physical world I live in. The evidence is there before my very eyes. I see a world full of extraordinary colour, diversity, creativity, order, beauty, wonder and life. The question is, if God created this beautiful world, why do we not see Him? Why does He remain hidden and out of sight? If He exists, what is stopping Him from making Himself known? Because of God's absence, our society does not believe in His existence; no God, no heaven and no hell. Once we die our death, we are dead in nothingness, and the meaning of life disappears.

The Western world is happy to live independently of God and get by without Him. It is happy to dismiss Him as something that belongs to the uncivilized, juvenile beliefs of the ancient, simplistic world. In the world of today, our advanced technology and sophisticated understanding have convinced us that we have progressed in our thinking so that there is no need for God. We look to science to provide the answers to a lot of our big questions. However, the scientific world cannot write off God or explain Him away. Without realizing it, science simply tries to work out how God put everything together and keeps it together. God is a God of the supernatural, and science cannot explain Him. How ironic that God created both the scientist and science! Evolutionists attempt to climb on the back of science to disprove the *need* for God to exist. They teach us that the world we live in came out of nothing and conclude that the world could not form itself into what it is overnight or in six days. This finding is perfectly true when God is taken out of the equation. To explain how everything came into existence, they use unproved methods that use the passing of time and good fortune to explain what has produced the variety and complexity of what we see today. In spite of the many unexplained gaps in their theory, evolution is taught as fact. The casualty in all of this is the Creator Himself, and His existence is denied. This falls right into the hands of the atheist, who might argue that if God does exist, then science would have discovered Him by now.

The atheist uses the absence of God to prove that He does not exist. Whilst proving to be God's biggest opponent, the atheist proves to be the Devil's greatest advocate. The atheist will throw everything that is evil against the suggestion of God's existence, accusing Him of being sadistic, immoral, vindictive, hateful, angry, power crazy, a despot dictator, cruel and thoroughly evil. If God is supposed to be so loving and omnipotent, why does He allow horrific suffering to take place and the innocent to suffer? If God does exist, they say, He is not a God of love but a God of injustice. They reason that those who believe in such a God are ignorant simpletons who have not thought these things through properly. Yet in taking this stance, the atheist sides with the Devil, who is the reality behind all such unbelief. Needless to say, the atheist does not believe in the existence of the Devil either.

The fact that God is absent does raise legitimate questions that deserve to be answered. Those answers will not satisfy everyone, and many refuse to believe that God exists simply because they do not *want* Him to exist.

As someone who has faith in God through Jesus Christ, His absence does not fill me with happiness but great sadness and grief. I wish He would show up and show Himself to the world and prove all the sceptics wrong! Yet the Bible gives an explanation for His absence. It teaches me that something huge is not right; something really big is wrong that has paved the way for a world that is full of evil and the absence of God.

The Spiritual Disease of Sin and Death

Even from conception, everyone has been infected by the most hideous disease that anyone could ever contract. The Bible calls this disease sin. It is a spiritual disease for which there is no human cure. It is the deadliest disease because of its devastating consequences. We are all born with this disease and its most damning effect is that it separates us from the presence of God, both in this life and the next. This disease is so devious, leaving most of its victims refusing to believe that they even have it. The proof that we have this spiritual disease is seen in our natural preference to live a life that is content to ignore God and live without Him. This is our natural state into which we are born, rendering us incapable of knowing God, let alone wanting to believe in Him.

Sin and evil are interconnected. They are married to each other. In themselves, evil and sin have no substance or form, which means that we cannot hold them or examine them under a microscope. The manifestation of sin is evil, corrupting everything that has been infected by it, including our minds and physical bodies. The only way to observe sin is by looking at the bad fruit it produces. The fruit of sin manifests itself through the body in so many different ways, the most obvious of which are evil acts, immorality, disobedience and not doing what is right and good. As I have already said, the essence of sin from which these things flow is to desire something more than we desire to know God. We desire to carry out our own will rather than the will of God, placing ourselves in the number one position rather than God. No matter how hard we might try to stay free from sin and its effects, we will never succeed. For example, no matter how hard any of us try to be perfect, our attempt will simply highlight the existence of our imperfections. No matter how much we dedicate ourselves to a strict regime that is designed to keep us physically fit and healthy, sin will soon ravage our entire body through sickness, old age and death. No one can escape this onslaught or win this battle. In every single case, sin destroys.

I am sure that you would agree that all of us will die a physical death and that none of us can do anything about it. On that day, no amount of money or good connections will make any difference. No matter how decent or nice we may have been, the enemy 'death' will make no distinction. No amount of 'Christian' burial or prayer petition can alter anything for anyone once they have died in their sin. To die in one's sin is really the worst thing that can happen to anyone since it marks the point of no return, no reprieve, no second chance.

The most devastating effect of our sin is not that we die physically but spiritually. Sin renders our spirit dead to God in this life and the next. For this, there is no human cure, and even the most accomplished medical experts the world has to offer have this disease themselves. The whole of the human race stands united in a predicament of total helplessness, incapable of finding a cure that will eliminate our common human dilemma. Even the death of our body does not eliminate the consequences of this spiritual death; in fact, physical death brings those consequences to a head, condemning a person to an eternity in a place the Bible calls the second death, lake of fire or hell (Rev. 2:11 – 20:6, 14 – 21:8). The second death is to be feared more than the first. The second death is God's eternal judgment that simply grants the sinner what they have already chosen to do and be in this life. The judgment of God gives the sinner over to their natural desire to live life without Him, and in that sense, God allows the sinner to condemn themselves. We might find this difficult to accept and hard to comprehend, but what it represents is the serious gravity of our sin and the enormous chasm it creates between us and a Holy God.

Jesus spoke of Judas Iscariot, who was one of His 12 disciples and who betrayed Him, saying that it would have been better for him never to have been born (Matt. 26:24). Jesus said this knowing that after Judas had experienced the death of His physical body, he would have to face up to the judgment of God and the second death that banishes him eternally from the presence of God. We can conclude from this that if a person dies in their sin, it would be better that they, too, had never been born in the first place. This is a terrifying prospect and something that demands our most urgent attention.

So many of us make every effort to keep the day of our death at a safe distance, yet we do nothing to avoid the second death. The irony is that none of us can avoid the first death, but we can take evasive action to avoid the second. Astonishingly, most of us do not. The greatest need that anyone will ever have in this life is to get right with God and so be freed from the condemnation of their sin and escape that second death.

I imagine that most people fear the *process* of dying more than death itself. If we had the power to request what kind of death we died, all of us would request a long prosperous life followed by a quick, dignified death through which we die peacefully in our sleep. Sadly, we do not always get our request. Death reflects the taking away of something good and precious, the destruction of the miracle of life that is so evident when a baby is first born.

Ignoring Sin and Death

We all die physically and spiritually because of the presence of sin in our lives. In our secular, sophisticated, entertainment-driven society, sin is a word to be laughed at and not taken seriously. We try to do the same with death. Increasingly in the West, we live as though there is no such thing as sin, yet sin is the reason why our bodies die. Most people ridicule the concept of sin and treat death as a taboo subject. These things do not fit in with our hopes and self-esteem. We overlook the fact that the cause of all death is sin. Therefore, nobody wants to be told the truth about their sin or be reminded of its presence or horrendous consequences. Consequently, society downplays the effects of sin as though only the really heinous sins matter. Thus, when most people die, we consider them to be good enough for heaven. We give them a Christian funeral as if this will serve them well as they move on to meet their maker. We trivialize death, believing the dead to be at rest and peace in a better place. None of these false hopes come from the Bible and are a reflection of our ignorance of the biblical truths.

The Origin of Sin

All of us are born into a sinful condition with a sinful nature. We inherit the sinful nature of Adam, who was the first human being to be created by God and the federal head of the entire human race. We were created *by* God and *for* God, to live in perfect harmony and communion with Him in the perfect world that He had created. In His wisdom, God commanded Adam not to eat the fruit of the tree of the knowledge of good and evil.

> *'The Lord God took the man and put him in the garden of Eden to work it and keep it. And the Lord God commanded the man, saying, "You may surely eat of every tree of the garden, but of the tree of the knowledge of good and evil you shall not eat, for in the day that you eat of it you shall surely die"'* (Gen. 2:15–17).

Eve, who God created from one of Adam's ribs and to be *'a helper fit for him,'* made the deadly error of listening to Satan's seduction who, in the form of a serpent, deceived her into eating the fruit, telling her:

> *'You will not surely die. For God knows that when you eat of it your eyes will be opened, and you will be like God, knowing good and evil. So when the woman saw that the tree was good for food, and that it was a delight to the eyes, and that the tree was to be desired to make one wise, she took of its fruit and ate, and she also gave some to her husband and he ate. Then the eyes of both were opened and they knew that they were naked'* (Gen. 3:4–7).

Eve was deceived by the serpent, who in turn seduced Adam, who as the God-given headship over Eve, should have known better and failed to demonstrate his headship. Both were enticed to believe Satan's lie that their disobedience would not bring them into harm, but instead enable them to become like God. This was nothing less than an act of deliberate, defiant rebellion against God that was nothing less than a demand for equality with God; to do what they saw fit to do in their own eyes. This is where sin was born, and their rebellion set them up against God who brought upon them His swift judgment, putting them to death spiritually, resulting in their separation from the oneness that they had previously enjoyed of living in union and harmony with God. Adam and Eve became the very first sinners; they were stuck with it and unable to shake it off. It was to be a noose around their necks and for the whole of humanity that followed after them.

The symptom of this sinful condition manifests itself by living for the honour and glory of ourselves rather than the honour and glory of God. It is a life that lives independently of God. Consequently, whether we realize it or not, it is a life that lives in rebellion and defiance against God, reflected by our inability to live in obedience to Him or for His glory. The thing that we really need to understand at this point is that God is extremely offended by our rebellion against Him, which is epitomized by our disobedience to the first and greatest God-given commandment:

'You shall have no other gods before me' (Ex. 20).

The consequence of dying in our sin does not lead to our resting in peace, as many suppose. Rather, our soul will spend eternity in a place totally separated from the presence of God and any of His goodness. The Bible calls this place hell. People today snigger at that word, and Christians often avoid using it for fear of losing their credibility, yet Jesus spoke more about hell than He did about heaven. Some choose to believe that hell is something that is limited to the really bad times experienced in the here and now:

hell, on earth. Others refuse to believe in a literal hell yet are only too happy to believe in a literal heaven. You may say that even if hell does exist as an eternal state, you will be happy to live there since you lived your earthly life separated from God's presence and were fine with that. However, Jesus described hell as a place of eternal torment, weeping and gnashing of teeth. There is nothing there that will reflect the goodness and perfection of God or His blessings. In this world, even though it has been so messed up by the presence of sin, there is still plenty of God's goodness, perfection and blessings to be seen and enjoyed in what He has created. In this life, whether we have faith or no faith, we all get tremendous enjoyment as we gaze and marvel at awesome scenery, a sunset, the sounds and sights of the animal kingdom, the beauty of plantation, flowers and so on: All of God's creation reflects His glorious splendour. Hell will be nothing like this world, which is so full of God's blessings and goodness; rather, anyone who finds themselves in hell will be horrified by their predicament. Not only is this so, but Satan and his demonic angels, who first brought sin into God's perfect world in the Garden of Eden, are assigned a place there by God. Jesus told us that hell is a place prepared for Satan and his evil demons (Matt. 25:41). All who die in this life still attached to their sin is simply going from bad to worse. Hell is the ultimate consequence of the spiritual disease of sin. Left to our own devices, this is the default destination for every human being who has ever lived. No one will be there unless they deserve to be there. The uncomfortable truth is that every single one of us deserves to be in hell and none of us deserves to be in heaven. No one can buy their way into heaven, and no one can buy their way out of hell.

The Day of Judgment

No one who finds themselves in hell will be able to contest the verdict, for there is a coming Day of Judgment where all the evidence of our rebellion against God will be made known. God sees and knows everything; nothing will be hidden and everything about us will be exposed. The Day of Judgment will be a Day of accountability and justice where all of the wrong we have committed against God in this life will be called to account.

The Apostle John writes:

> *'Then I saw a great white throne and him who was seated on it. From his presence earth and sky fled away, and no place was found for them. And I saw the dead, great and small, standing before the throne, and books were opened. Then another book was opened, which is the book of life. And the dead were judged by what was written in the books, according to what they had done. And the sea gave up the dead who were in it, Death and Hades gave up the dead who were in them, and they were judged, each one of them, according to what they had done. Then Death and Hades were thrown into the lake of fire. This is the second death, the lake of fire. And if anyone's name was not found written in the book of life, he was thrown into the lake of fire'* (Rev. 20:11–15).

On that Day of Judgment, every person's eternal destiny will be made known and fixed. It will not be decided by whatever we have achieved, owned or stood for in life. No matter how successful, wealthy, influential, likeable, kind, nice or generous we have been, we cannot use these things to impress God or cancel out our disobedience against Him. On that Day, God will not be persuaded, coerced, bribed, bought, hoodwinked or deceived. Only one thing will determine our eternal destiny on that Day, and that will be whether or not we have died in our sin.

Therefore, the most dangerous way for anyone to live this life is to live it independently of God, which is the breaking of the 1st Commandment. Just as with Adam, God sees this as an act of rebellion against Him. Therefore, the worst thing that can happen to us in this life is that we die in our sin. If we die in our sin, the guilt of our sin remains upon us, and God will judge us accordingly on the Day of Judgment. The verdict of guilty will be reached, and God will sentence the sinner to an eternal place whereupon the condemnation of our sin remains upon us forever. This is no nightclub. The Bible describes this place as the second death, where a person will perish, yet will not cease to exist. Once a person had been locked into the second death, there will be no going back or second chance.

People laugh at the whole concept of hell, but it will be no laughing matter on that Day of Judgment. I cringe when I hear people joke that they would rather spend eternity in hell, reasoning that it will be much more fun than floating around on clouds in the heavenlies playing harps. This deluded, childish perception has nothing to do with the biblical concepts of heaven or hell. Jesus never described heaven in that way, and He did not describe hell as a fun place to be. None of us can afford to laugh at the words of Jesus, for He claimed to be the truth and always told the truth.

Is there a way for us to be saved from such a horrific future? Now, at long last, here comes the good news. No one can escape the first death, but the Bible teaches us that God has provided the way for us to escape the second death.

Chapter 3

THE CROSS OF JESUS CHRIST

The Good News

The good news of Jesus Christ takes us to the cross of Jesus from where God reveals at least two things:

1. The grievous offence of our sin against Holy God that deserves His eternal wrath and judgment.
2. The incredible demonstration of God's love, to save us eternally from our sin.

I had to explain the bad news first, otherwise the good news makes no sense at all. The good news is incredibly good and tells us that there is a way of escape! The Bible teaches that, as a demonstration of His love, God has provided a way for us to be freed from the guilt of our sin in this life, meaning that we will not die in our sin or face the Day of Judgment. The result is that our eternal destiny is not the second death but rather eternal life. John 3:16 teaches us that:

> *For God so loved the world, that He gave us his only Son, that whoever believes in him* [Jesus] *will not perish but have eternal life.'*

What Jesus Accomplished

The justice of God's Holy righteousness cannot overlook or sweep sin under the carpet and demands that all who sin against Him must die. The Bible teaches us that *'The wages of sin is death'* and *'All have sinned and fall short of the glory of God'* (Rom. 3:23 & 6:23).

God's justice demands that all sin is judged and that sinners pay the price for their own rebellion against His holiness and standards. This will take place on the Day of Judgment at the end of human history. Yet that same justice has provided the means by which the sinners' penalty can be paid for by someone else *before* the arrival of the Day of Judgment. This has been God's determined plan even before Adam first sinned. As the first human being that God created, Adam personified the head of the entire human race and, through his rebellion against God, brought condemnation to both himself and all of humanity that emanated from his seed. Yet God has provided a redeemer who personified the whole of humanity. This redeemer had to come from within the human race in order to act on their behalf by paying the price to set them free from their condemnation. To qualify for such a task, the redeemer had to meet God's Holy standards and someone who had committed no sin of their own. Needless to say, no such person born of Adam has ever existed. To solve this seemingly unsurmountable problem, God in His love set out to provide the solution by sending His only Son from heaven to earth, to be born into humanity and become one of us. Hence, the Holy Spirit came upon the Virgin Mary in the land of Israel, who conceived and gave birth to the baby boy Jesus, the only baby in history to be born without sin.

Jesus lived the first 30 years of His life as an ordinary Jew and committed no sin. Not once did He live independently of His Father in heaven or rebel against Him but lived entirely to do His Father's will. At the age of about 30, Jesus began to tell people who He really was, where He had come from and why. He began to teach about His Father in heaven and about the kingdom of God. He began to meet the physical needs of the people by healing their sicknesses, making the lame walk, the blind see, the deaf hear and raise some people from the dead who had recently died. All of these miraculous healings served to demonstrate that Jesus had come to do a greater good, which was to heal people of their spiritual sickness, sin.

Even so, the Jewish religious leaders hated Jesus, rejecting Him as their Messiah while accusing Him of blasphemy against Yahweh, the God of Israel. They condemned Him as a guilty criminal worthy of death. At the age of 33, the sinless Jesus found Himself being crucified to death by Roman soldiers on a cross of bloody execution (AD 30).

Had Jesus failed to do what He came to do? Far from it, for God sent His Son into the world in order for Him to go the cross, a place Jesus could have so easily avoided, but He took Himself there in full obedience to carry out His Father's will. At the cross, the sinless Jesus took upon Himself our sin, and so God declared the innocent Jesus to be guilty of our sin. At the cross, Jesus took upon Himself the full force of God's judgment, substituting Himself for the sinner. At the cross, a great exchange took place, whereby Jesus took upon Himself the sinner's sin and imputed to the sinner His perfect righteousness. Through what Jesus accomplished at the cross, the sinner is justified before God and declared completely innocent of their sin. Jesus paid the price in full on the sinner's behalf.

The Apostle Paul writes:

'For our sake He made him to be sin who knew no sin, so that in him we might become the righteousness of God' (2 Cor. 5:21).

Just before He died and knowing that He would rise from the dead three days later, Jesus cried out, 'It is finished,' indicating the end of His salvific work that God had sent Him to carry out. Such justification paves the way for God to forgive us of our rebellion against Him. God did not do this because any of us deserve it, but because He chose to demonstrate His love and mercy over us. In doing so, God in Jesus met our most desperate need in life, a need that no one else could meet, including ourselves. The selfless, substitutionary sacrifice of Jesus means that the forgiven, justified sinner will be raised from the dead at a future date, not for the Day of Judgment followed by hell, but to enter into the eternal kingdom of God.

Necessity to Respond

Is that it? No, this does not reveal the whole picture. Before any of us can be freed from the condemnation of our sin and receive the gift of salvation, a condition must be met. The justice of God *demands* the sinner give God the response He is looking for, without which nothing that Christ accomplished at the cross can be accredited to us. That response can only be made once our eyes have first been opened by God in response to the hearing of the gospel message of Jesus, which is the good news that is Jesus. As the Apostle Paul wrote: '*So faith comes from hearing, and hearing through the word of Christ*' (Rom. 10:17). It's not so much that we simply make the *decision* to respond but that we are *convicted* to respond by the crushing awareness of our guilt before a Holy God. How are we to respond? We respond by *repenting* of our sin and *believing* in Jesus. We repent by acknowledging and confessing our sin against God with a deep sorrow that calls upon God to forgive us, a sorrow and regret that recognizes how we have lived independently of Him, and therefore in rebellion and rightly deserving to be judged by Him. True repentance compels us to turn away from our sin and turn to God. Having repented, we also need to believe in Jesus. To believe is not just to believe in the historical Jesus, or that He died on a cross, was raised back to life and then ascended into heaven where He was before. While these things are extremely important, the faith that saves is to believe in what Jesus *accomplished* at the cross on our behalf, where He justified us before God and paved the way for God to forgive us of our sin against Him. This is what it means to put our faith in Jesus as we trust in Him to save us from our sin. If our repentance and belief is authentic, the sinner will not perish, but have everlasting life in God's glorious goodness and perfection. This is the good news that is Jesus Christ, who completes, secures and guarantees our eternal redemption.

Salvation from sin is a free love gift from God. It cannot be bought or earned but is freely given by God to all who will repent and believe. The gift is there for our taking, yet remember this; we can only call upon the name of the Lord Jesus and receive this precious gift *this* side of death. The good news is astonishingly good! An earthly inheritance is short-lived, lasting only until one's death, at which point it all becomes meaningless and worthless. The good news of salvation in Jesus provides a heavenly inheritance that will last for the whole of eternity. Jesus said:

> '*If anyone would come after me, let him deny himself and take up his cross and follow me. For whoever would save his life will lose it, but whoever loses his life for my sake and the gospel's will save it. For what does it profit a man to gain the whole world and forfeit his soul? For what can a man give in return for his soul?*' (Mark 8:34–37).

Chapter 4

A NEW LIFE

Jesus did not deserve to be put to death since He was totally innocent of any crime. Three days after His death and burial, the same justice that demanded the substitutionary death of Jesus also demanded His vindication by raising Him bodily back to life. Jesus walked out of His tomb, leaving it empty apart from His grave clothes. The bodily resurrection of Jesus revealed that the justice of God was satisfied and that the substitutionary atonement made by Jesus on the sinner's behalf was wholly acceptable to God. The resurrection of Jesus paves the way for our own bodily resurrection at the return of Jesus from heaven to earth. Yet there is a resurrection to be experienced the moment we repent and believe, a *spiritual* resurrection through which we get to live a new life in the here and now. This is not so much what *we* choose to do but *God* chooses to do; we do not choose God, but He chooses us. God calls us to Himself through the convicting work of the Holy Spirit, who brings us into a place of genuine repentance and faith in Jesus. At this point, God performs a supernatural miracle whereby He places His Holy Spirit within us, empowering us to undergo a spiritual rebirth from out of the world and into the kingdom of God. Through spiritual rebirth, our spirit is made alive to God, meaning that we are no longer spiritually dead or alienated from Him. We have become a new creation, empowered by the Holy Spirit to live a new life that *wants* to know God and worship Him with life itself. This new life produces a new desire and a heavenly mindset that sets out to seek first the kingdom of God and His righteousness (see Matt. 6:32–34).

It is a new life of transformation that surrenders to the Lordship of Jesus Christ. It is a new life that allows God to speak into our lives as we study the Bible. It is through the Bible that the Holy Spirit brings us into a greater knowledge and understanding of who God is and the salvation we have in Jesus Christ. This new life lives in the joy of our salvation, providing us with tremendous peace, rest and a joyful expectation of what is yet to come. When our natural life ends and we find ourselves standing before Jesus, we will be so full of joy to finally see the one who took away our sin and enabled us to live with hope and full assurance. On the day we stand before Jesus, we will grasp the full force of God's mercy and love by which we enter into an everlasting life of worship in the fullness of God's goodness and presence. Until then, we continue to live in a fallen world, a fallen body, surrounded by the presence of sin where bad things still happen. Even as a new creation, we will fight a daily battle against the fleshly desires of our own sinful nature that belongs to the old creation, yet we do so bearing faithful witness and testimony to the salvation we have in Jesus.

Most people consider themselves to be decent human beings who have, on the whole, lived life as a good person. This assessment is made since they reckon that their goodness far outweighs their badness. Yet the cross of Jesus reminds each one of us that no one is good enough for heaven, but everyone is bad enough for hell. No one deserves heaven, but everyone deserves hell. That is a judgment that no one can protest against, since it is the judgment made by God who demands absolute perfection and goodness all of the time. For the one who has become a new creation, that demand is fully met in Christ as they continue to live in faith and trust in Him.

At the cross, the whole of humanity is levelled. It makes no difference who you are; you might be black or white, young or old, healthy or sick, an outstanding law-abiding citizen or a malicious villain. You might be filthy rich or devastatingly poor, influential or a nobody. You might be intelligent or ignorant, of high rank or low standing, successful or a failure. You might believe that Jesus existed or that He never did. It makes no difference. As with death itself, the cross of Jesus brings each one of us down to the same level, placing us all on an equal footing. In the eyes of God, each one of us, without exception, stands before the cross of Jesus as a convicted, condemned criminal because each one of us has broken the Laws of God by our sinful acts and our sinful thinking. Here's the thing; the cross is designed not to condemn us but to save us, restoring us into a right relationship with God.

God is Love

A lot of people find the message of the cross offensive and foolish. Many Christians are really uncomfortable with the side of God that displays His wrath and judgment, and so they dumb these things down at Easter time by beautifying the cross with flowers, Easter eggs and bunny rabbits. The truth is, God does not have different sides to His character. He is a God of wrath *and* mercy, judgment *and* love, all at the same time. While the cross most certainly demonstrates the wrath of God against sin, it equally demonstrates His love to save the repentant sinner from their sin. At the cross, God has provided a way for us to be delivered from the power of sin's condemnation, regardless of who we are.

Why Can't God Simply Forgive Everyone?

If God is so powerful and loving, what is to stop Him from forgiving the whole of the human race of their sin since Jesus has already paid the price for our sin? Here's the thing, if God were to allow for that, He would no longer be good or Holy. A lot of Christian posters placed outside church buildings seem to suggest that God forgives everyone, yet the Bible never teaches this. Posters that say 'God loves you' or 'Jesus died to save you' can be very misleading to someone who is not a Christian. While these posters do speak the truth, it is not the whole truth. Someone might take those words as an assurance that means if God exists, they will be fine because He loves them, has saved them, and accepts them as they are without them having to face up to and confess their own sin. The cross is where God's rescue mission took place and each one of us has a choice: Either we take ourselves to Jesus at the cross where we are rescued from our sin and the judgment of God, or we reject Jesus and take the full force of God's wrath on the Day of Judgment.

No Escape from God's Judgment

The Bible teaches that at the end of human history, every unrepentant sinner will face the judgment of God. From this there is no escape. In John 5:22, Jesus says: *'For the Father judges no one, but has given all judgment to the Son,'* and Acts 17:31 tells us that God *'...has fixed a day on which he will judge the world in righteousness by a man whom he has appointed; and of this he has given assurance to all by raising him from the dead.'*

Since Jesus is both fully God and fully human, He is well qualified to represent God and judge the whole of humanity. His judgment will determine the degree of punishment for those who have not repented of their sin or put their faith in Him (Luke 12: 47–48). This punishment will be served in that eternal place that is completely devoid of the presence of God or any of His goodness. This place of no return is called the lake of fire or the second death (Rev. 20:11-15). The Bible also speaks of the Judgment seat of Christ, but this has nothing to do with the Day of Judgment that is reserved for unrepentant sinners. The Apostle Paul, writing to Christians teaches:

'For we must all appear before the judgment seat of Christ, so that each one may receive what is due for what He has done in the body, whether good or evil' (2 Cor. 5:10).

This judgment is not to punish but to reward believers according to their works of service to God. The bottom line is that Jesus will either be our Saviour or our Judge.

Understanding the Bad News and the Good News

No one can ever understand the good news of salvation in Jesus unless we first understand the bad news of God's judgment upon sin. If we are not made aware of the bad news first, we will not understand our most desperate need to repent of our sin and what Jesus saves us *from* and *for*. Much of modern-day evangelism skips the bad news and jumps straight in with the good news. It avoids the bad news for fear that the bad news is too negative and judgemental. The last thing such evangelism wants is to put people off before they get the chance to hear that Jesus loves them so much. Such evangelism says the good news is that Jesus loves everyone unconditionally and wants to be their friend; all one has to do is accept Jesus into their heart and He will welcome them into His eternal kingdom. Much of modern-day Christianity does not like the God we read about in the Old Testament and shy away from Him. They do not like this God who gets angry and is full of wrath. Who wants to believe in such a bad God? Give me a good God who will accept everything about me and make me feel so special and lovable. As I have already said, if God did such a thing, He would no longer be good or Holy. Unfortunately, many Christians today are embarrassed by the God of the OT and feel the need to apologize for His past bad behaviour. For many Christians, the God of the NT is far more acceptable because He is now full of love and grace. This discrepancy is not what the Bible teaches. God's character is always consistent and never changes. In both the OT and NT, God is revealed as both a God of wrath who judges sin *and* a God of love who saves people from their sin.

Chapter 5

THE PRESENCE OF THE HOLY SPIRIT

Through the atonement of Jesus, God forgives us our sin and reconciles us to Himself, removing the barrier of sin that separated us from Him. Such reconciliation opens up the door to know the presence of God in this life. This knowing, even at its best, is a rather veiled and dim reflection compared to the glorious and complete unveiling of God's presence which we will experience beyond this life. For those who put their faith in Christ, God has *partially* lifted the veil, meaning that we are no longer spiritually blind or deaf to God. With eyes and ears of faith, we see and hear God, especially through His written word in the Bible. The reason for this dramatic shift is that God places His Holy Spirit into every true believer the moment the Spirit opens their understanding to the good news that is Jesus, so they can genuinely repent and believe. The Holy Spirit performs this supernatural miracle that leads to nothing less than our spiritual rebirth, through which we are born from out of this world and into the kingdom of God and adopted into His family. Thus, we become a new creation that longs to know the presence of God with us. I know that one day in the future, I will live in the fullness of His presence when He takes me home to be with Him in heaven. On that day, and for the first time ever, I will experience a total separation from the presence of sin, this fallen world and my fallen body. In the meantime, I am still here, yet the Bible teaches me that the presence of God abides in me today through the indwelling Holy Spirit, who empowers, equips, strengthens and encourages me in my journey of faith.

God has given me His Spirit to enable me to live in faithfulness to Him and to the testimony of salvation I have in Jesus. I fail to comprehend how astonishing it is that Jesus has placed His Holy presence within me through the Holy Spirit. I am so desperate to see that truth become a daily reality, where I experience a greater evidence and demonstration of His presence with me; His presence to heal, restore and save! God's presence cannot be organized, manufactured or manipulated; it can only be received as a gift of God's grace.

I know that without the Holy Spirit, I cannot be born into the kingdom of God and am left powerless to follow Jesus or live the Christian life. Without the enlightenment of the Spirit, I cannot understand the spiritual truths of what the Bible teaches or bear an effective witness to the salvation I have in Jesus. It is the Spirit who equips me to worship God from my heart, in spirit and truth, word or deed. It is the Spirit who causes me to hunger after God, to diligently seek Him, His kingdom and His righteousness. It is by the Spirit that I have communion and fellowship with Jesus, since it is the Spirit who unites me to God the Son and God the Father.

The Breaking of Sin's Power

Receiving the gift of the Holy Spirit provides me with a new mindset, dramatically changing my whole outlook on this life. I can now live the rest of my life in the security of knowing that through Christ, I have been set free from the power of sin. That is a huge burden lifted that paves the way for me to enjoy the joy of my salvation.

Before sin's power and hold over me was broken, I was a slave to sin and dead to God. I had no desire to know Him or get right with Him. When the power of sin over me was broken, I was compelled by the Spirit to *want* to know God more. There is a draw towards God that was not there before, and it is has been put there by the Spirit. The separation from God that I previously experienced has been removed and the way into God's presence opened up.

Before sin's power and hold over me was broken, my life was really all about me. It was *my* life, it belonged to me. I was number one because I lived to serve *my* interests. Today we live in a culture that thrives on me-ism and selfishness. Through faith in Jesus, the Spirit shifts the focus from belief in self to belief in Jesus. It is the Spirit who brings about this transformation of the heart, empowering us to die to the desires of the flesh and to this world. It is a death where we no longer live for this world because the world no longer holds any appeal. As for me, I am but a stranger and alien who is merely passing through, seeing beyond this life, and living for the life to come. This dying is a worthy death since it gives rise for the eternal life of Jesus to live in me.

God sent Jesus into this world to save sinners from their sin; I am one of those sinners. He did this that I may live for His honour and glory, not my own. I am no longer enslaved by the power of sin's condemnation, but am placed under, and protected by, the power and authority of Jesus. This salvation cannot be destroyed by cancer. My salvation in Jesus will outlive my cancer. Therefore, my hope is not in this world or even in my physical healing but in what follows. My hope is in Jesus, who cancels out the power of cancer, death and sin.

Chapter 6

THE IMPORTANCE OF FAITH

Faith is Priceless

The Bible teaches me that faith is more precious than gold (1 Peter 1:7). Why is it considered to be so valuable? Peter tells us why in verse 9, telling us that the outcome of our faith is the salvation of our souls. What would you pay for something that you knew could buy you eternal life in a location which could only be described as Paradise? In Paradise, everything is perfect and full of happiness, a place where there is no such thing as death, illness, old age, hatred, corruption and the like. Your place in Paradise cannot be won, earned or purchased in any way. It can only be *given* to you as a free gift. What is more, it is Paradise because God is there in all of His unveiled fullness, goodness and glory. If God were not there, it would not be Paradise. Faith in Jesus paves the way for Paradise.

Faith in Jesus is so important that Jesus told His followers to go and make more followers who will put their faith in Him. This has been the primary commission that Jesus has given to His church prior to His ascension back into heaven and His future return. This is the commission of proclaiming the good news of Jesus to those who need to hear. Jesus did not commission His followers to proclaim a cause, philosophy, institution, religion or social gospel. These things may very well bring some good changes to a person's life, but they do not have the power to save anyone from their sin against God. Jesus did not tell His followers to go and save the planet, He told them to go and tell the world about Himself, because He is the only one who can provide the salvation we all so desperately need. Jesus is the only one who can get rid of the bad and restore what is good. God sent the good news from heaven to earth to meet the world's most desperate need, a need that only Jesus can meet.

What is Faith?

The dictionary tells me that faith means having a strong belief in something based on conviction rather than proof. It can also mean to have complete trust or confidence in something or someone. Throughout the world there are many different faiths and beliefs. For example, Hinduism believes in 33 million gods. Muslims believe in one god, Allah, while atheists and humanists hold to a belief that there is no God. Apart from orthodox Christianity, all other religions that believe in some kind of afterlife teach that salvation must be earned by doing good works or performing certain rituals.

I hold to a belief that there is only one God, the God revealed to us in the pages of the Bible. Through this God, I am unashamedly a Christian and don't care if I am ridiculed. I am proud to identify myself with the title Jesus has, which is Christ. These days, the label 'Christian' means so many things to different people. Many say they are a Christian because they go to a church, were raised in a so-called Christian country, consider themselves to be a good person or were christened as a baby. Some say they are a Christian Buddhist, the result of which comes from the increasingly popular idea of syncretism, which promotes the mixing of different religions, ideologies and philosophies. The Bible does not teach this but rather warns against it.

We cannot see faith with our eyes; it is invisible, having no physical substance. Faith only becomes tangible and given substance as it is lived out. Faith is seen by the impact it has upon a person's life. Faith does not exist in isolation to itself; it has to be placed in something or someone for it to mean anything. Christians do not hang a picture of Jesus Christ on the wall and pray to it; that is not faith but superstition. Instead, Christians hang their faith on the Jesus who is alive and lives in heaven.

The Bible Teaches:

> *'And without faith it is impossible to please him, for whoever would draw near to God must believe that he exists and that he rewards those who earnestly seek him'* (Heb. 11:6).

If I do not believe in God, then it is impossible for me to put my faith in him. It is relatively easy to put my faith in something or someone I can see, touch and know, but how am I to put my complete trust and confidence in something or someone I have never even met? What proof do I have that God is someone I can put my complete trust and confidence in? Even if I could, why should I? What do I stand to gain?

The question to be asked is, what do I stand to lose if I do not put my faith in God? Many people shy away from all things 'God'. They see God as a spoilsport who insists they lose all their enjoyment in life and adhere to a set of controlling rules and regulations that restrict their freedom and sovereignty. Others believe in a God whose only demand upon them is that they live a good life. To stay in His good books, they appease Him by going to church once a week as though this acts as a weekly payment for an insurance policy that protects them from hell and guarantees them a safe place in heaven. Jesus once said:

> *"'Not everyone who says to me, 'Lord, Lord,' will enter the kingdom of heaven, but the one who does the will of my Father who is in heaven. On that day many will say to me, 'Lord, Lord, did we not prophesy in your name and cast out demons in your name, and do many mighty works in your name?' And then I will declare to them, 'I never knew you; depart from me, you workers of lawlessness'"* (Matt. 7:21–23).

On the Day of Judgment, there will be many people who presume they have a faith that protects them from hell and grants them access into heaven. Those 'many' people in the verse above sound as if they have enough faith in Jesus to prophesy and perform many miracles in His name. It must be reasonable to assume that their religious acts lead them to believe that if there is a heaven, they are sure to go there. Jesus debunks that assumption by telling us that on 'that Day' they will get the shock of their lives, not by the reality of heaven, but that they will be refused entry into it! Such false converts simply use faith as a superstitious tool that grants them entry into the kingdom of heaven, discovering that they have deluded themselves and that their faith has no meaning, no substance and no foundation in the Jesus that Scripture speaks of. A true faith that saves is one that lives to love Christ more than self and expresses that love by living in obedience to His commands and doing His will.

Faith Reconciles Me to God

Faith is given birth at the cross of Christ. Faith begins by believing what Jesus accomplished at the cross on my behalf. He took my sin and, in return, accredited to me His righteousness so that I now stand justified before God. I therefore live with the assurance that, in Jesus, God *accepts* me and has forgiven me of my sin. It is not so much that I have accepted God, but that God has accepted me. Even though cancer has sentenced my body to death, I have nothing to fear because I know that I have had my greatest ever need met, which is to be reconciled to God in Jesus.

All of us have basic essential daily needs that need to be met, such as food, water, clothes, money and shelter. Today, most of us in the West have extended those essential needs to include luxury items such as cars, houses, holidays, entertainment, electronics and the like. The thing is, we will need none of those essential things on the day of our death, but rather, there is only one thing that we will need, which is the righteousness of Christ that He imputes to us.

Is Faith Happiness?

Since faith in Jesus reconciles me to God, does that mean I should be full of happiness all of the time? Not necessarily. I see plenty of people who seem to be full of happiness but have no faith. Jesus Himself was full of faith yet was not full of happiness all of the time:

> *'For he grew up before him like a young plant, and like a root out of a dry ground; he had no form or majesty that we should look at him, and no beauty that we should desire him. He was despised and rejected by men, a man of sorrows and acquainted with grief; and as one from whom men hide their faces he was despised, and we esteemed him not'* (Isa. 53:2–3).

In the Garden of Gethsemane, where Jesus spent His last night knowing that He was about to be betrayed, arrested, led away and crucified, He agonized in prayer to His heavenly Father.

Speaking of this occasion, Luke writes:

> *'And being in agony he prayed more earnestly; and his sweat became like great drops of blood falling down to the ground'* (Luke 22:44).

Sweating blood is a condition that is medically recognized as 'Hematidrosis' and can occur under immense stress and anxiety. Jesus was about to take the full weight and burden of our sin upon Himself, exposing Himself to the full force of God's judgment and justice. Yet we know that, even during that awful night of anticipating His dreadful execution and separation from God His Father, Jesus possessed a joy as He looked ahead beyond the anguish of His impending sacrifice. Talking of Jesus, the writer of Hebrews writes:

> *'...who for the joy that was set before him endured the cross'* (Heb.12:2).

You and I can go through the most painful, confusing, testing time and yet still be full of faith and full of the joy of our salvation. That joy comes through knowing Jesus as Lord of our mind, body and soul. He is the source of our joy and salvation, which is not based on how happy we feel but by our faith and confidence in Jesus.

If we suffer because of persecution, we might say that we are happy to suffer for the sake of Christ and to be considered worthy to do so. However, the suffering I am going through has nothing to do with persecution, and so I cannot consider myself worthy to suffer cancer for the sake of Christ. Nevertheless, I can still find joy in the predicament of my illness while doing everything I can to protect myself from being robbed of that joy. How do I do that? I do that by continuing to fix my eyes on Jesus, taking refuge in Him and abiding in Him. The Christians of today's Christianized West (and I include myself) have no idea what it means to stand up for our faith and suffer persecution. Instead, the church has grown accustomed to her acceptance by a society that has both respected and tolerated her for centuries. This has encouraged the church of recent decades to expect to live a comfortable, safe existence that supports nominal Christianity and a superficial, shallow faith. However, in our increasingly godless, secular society, significant changes are already taking place at a rapid pace. Long entrenched Christian values are already being eroded and no longer deemed acceptable by the powerful minority that insists on dictating to the majority. It is only a matter of time before an intolerant progressive culture demand that the uncompromising church be ostracized, shut down and outlawed. The same fate will apply to the Bible, which will be deemed to be an offensive book that promotes hate speech and must be 'cancelled out!' When the persecution of true Christians begins in England, and it will, the cost of being a true follower of Christ will rob nominal Christians of their comfort, leading them into apostasy and the abandonment of authentic faith and the narrow way that leads to life.

Our lives are not all about us or even about our happiness; it is about Jesus and our witness to His incredible salvation and the sufficiency of His grace. As we continue to live in a fallen world and fallen bodies, we continue to bear that witness, understanding that salvation is not personally realized until a person comes to the end of themselves and dies to this world. Until this dying takes place, we cannot truly surrender our all to Jesus and be satisfied in Him.

One Faith

While the world has many different faith religions, the Bible teaches there is only one authentic faith. This claim is made because the Bible teaches that there is only one person who can save us from our sin: Jesus. We get to live out that one faith with the one life that is given to each of us. That one life is made up of many different circumstances, challenges, places, seasons and choices. Our life presents us with one journey to be travelled, a journey where we get to apply and bear witness to that one faith.

How do We Get Faith?

The Bible teaches us how we get faith:

> '*For everyone who calls upon the name of the Lord will be saved. How then will they call on him in whom they have not believed? And how are they to believe in him of whom they have never heard? And how are they to hear without someone preaching? And how are they to preach unless they are sent? As it is written, " How beautiful are the feet of those who preach the good news!" '*(Rom. 10:13–15).

> '*So faith comes from hearing, and hearing through the word of Christ'*(Rom. 10:17).

The good news takes us to the cross of Jesus, where we are faced with both the reality of our sin and the salvation from sin that only Jesus can provide. This is where faith is born. We cannot buy, earn, create or inherit faith. Faith is given to us by God as a gift of His grace once we hear, receive, understand, repent and respond to the knowledge of the salvation that comes through Jesus Christ. The source of that knowledge is revealed in the Bible. That knowledge means nothing to us unless we believe it to be true. We cannot believe it to be true unless we believe that the Bible is the inspired word of God that carries with it the authority of God. Through His word we are confronted with the truth about ourselves, that we are sinners whose greatest need is to be made right with God. The Bible points and leads us to Jesus and the salvation from sin that only He can provide. Faith is given birth as we identify and unite ourselves with Jesus in both His death and bodily resurrection. That faith is not a subjective, gooey feeling but rather a rock-solid objective belief given to us by God.

Faith is Given and Received

Faith is not earned, it is given. The only one who can give faith is God, and it needs to be personally received. It is given as we respond to the message of God's salvation through what Jesus has accomplished at the cross on our behalf. The Holy Spirit convicts us to repent, giving to us the faith to believe in Jesus and equip us to live that faith out. Once received, we must cooperate with the Spirit by fanning into flame the faith that God has given to us, doing everything we can to protect, nurture and feed that faith. No one else can do that for you. It is a personal privilege and responsibility, yet impossible to do without the aid of the Holy Spirit.

Faith: For Better or Worse

Faith is the demonstration and expression of our being united to Jesus. Through faith we express our love for Jesus. Just as there is a honeymoon period in any new marriage, so too, there is a honeymoon period when a person first places their faith in Jesus. During this time, we might have great excitement and expectations, yet this period gradually comes to an end as reality kicks in. We begin to discover what faith really is and what we have signed up for. As with marriage, the ending of the honeymoon period paves the way for our faith to be stretched and put to the test. When our faith is put to the test, our love for Jesus is being tested, and we begin to understand that our relationship with Him needs to be worked at. With the honeymoon period behind us, we begin to recognize that being united to Jesus necessitates so much more than being given a baptismal certificate and the making of a one-off confession that says I do. Faith is a life-long commitment to Jesus that is determined to last the distance, for better or worse, in sickness and in health, richer or poorer. Along the way, we will be required to make personal sacrifices as we learn to place the interests of Jesus above our own. As with marriage, faith in Jesus is a relationship that involves a two-way commitment. As with marriage, the union of our faith in Jesus grows as we learn to give ourselves to Him in prayer and making time to study God's word. Reading the word of God is a bit like reading a marriage contract. It tells us of the promises God has made to us in Jesus and of His faithfulness and commitment to us. It is both encouraging yet challenging as we begin to grasp what Christ demands of us as we continue to unite ourselves to Him. The Bible speaks of the church as the bride of Christ and Christ as the Bridegroom of the church.

Faith Defines Who I Am

Faith is not something to be added on to our lives as some kind of statement or fashion accessory; rather, it is to be the very substance of our life and being. What defines me as a person is not that I am a 56-year-old man, husband, father or pastor. These things simply describe *who* I am. What defines me as a person is my identification with Jesus. It is who I am in Christ that defines my purpose in life and my reason for living.

Faith Determines My Whole Outlook on Life

Faith is not something that simply gives me a ticket to heaven when I die. True faith affects how I live my life, determining everything I do, say and think. It governs my whole outlook on both life and death. The depth and quality of my faith defines my worship, obedience and love for God, including my devotion to prayer and the study of God's word. Finding God is not a one-off event but an ongoing, life-long commitment that seeks to know more of God. This cannot fail to transform the way I live, think and the things I desire. Jesus is not just for Sundays, Easter or Christmas, but a way of life.

Faith Prepares Me for the Unexpected and Death

Come what may, the day of our death is certain to take place. We do not know how or when. You might be thinking how morbid; why think about such doom and gloom? Yet this proves my point that we are so reluctant to face up to the reality of death. We ignore it at our peril, for when the unexpected arrives, we will find ourselves unprepared. Most of us do not expect to die before reaching a certain age, yet we know it can come at any time and in any place. When it does arrive, it seems to shock us and take us by surprise.

'What is your life? For you are a mist that appears for a little time and then vanishes' (James 4:14).

Faith in Christ prepares me to face up to death in a way that sweeps away its doom, gloom and defeat. Faith in Christ provides me with the certainty that the death of my body paves the way for its resurrection and a future heavenly inheritance, a future that lives in the presence of God for all eternity.

'Behold, the dwelling place of God is with man. He will dwell with them, and they will be his people, and God himself will be with them as their God. He will wipe away every tear from their eyes, and death shall be no

46

more, neither shall there be mourning, nor crying, nor pain anymore, for the former things have passed away' (Rev. 21:3–4).

The day I was diagnosed with terminal cancer in 2016, I experienced for a second time the unexpected in a life-shattering way. On that day, I received the sentence of death to my health and body as the medical profession informed me that I was going to lose my life. The first occasion occurred in 1992, a day when the shock of the unexpected brought me to the end of myself. That day lasted two years, a period I call my Desert Place, when I experienced the loss of everything except my health.

These two trials are very different yet have significant similarities. Both of them have helped me to understand that faith must be prepared to lose everything. Suffering the loss of all things brings into focus just how precious faith is. When we lose everything, we begin to see what is important and what is not, what has meaningful value and what does not, what is temporal and what is eternal. The personal experience of losing everything has enabled me to better understand the value of faith in a way that reading Christian books, attending Christian conferences or listening to sermons could never do. Both trials have enforced the death of 'me' and the surrender of all to Jesus. Both of these trials have produced a faith in which I have learnt to expect the unexpected and the necessity of trusting in God. Such trust looks forward with great expectation to the resurrection of my redeemed body, which Jesus will give to me when He returns. Jesus said:

'I am the resurrection and the life. The one who believes in me will live, even though they die; and everyone who lives and believes in me shall never die' (John 11:25–26).

When Faith Does Not Seem to Work

When the road of faith we travel is blasted away by a gigantic bomb that leaves a huge crater, our faith is put to the test. To get us through this test, we need to have all the faith we can get. If we are to press on and reach our goal, our faith must be strengthened and encouraged.

True faith not only trusts but also prays. A huge bomb that appears to have destroyed our road is designed by God to send us to our knees in prayer. We throw ourselves at God's mercy in desperation, praying fervently for His deliverance and help. We pray with many tears, praying prayers that we know God can answer. We are often left to question why our prayers for deliverance do not work. The more we pray, the more it appears that our prayers make no difference, and we are left floundering in the aftermath, dazed and confused. I would like to think that when I have prayed my impassioned prayers, everything is going to be quickly resolved and the road repaired so that my journey can continue once again. However, experience teaches me that this is not always the case. Far from it. I have concluded that the bombs that explode on our road and the devastating depressions they leave are all part of the journey. They are not so much obstacles to be avoided but an integral part of the journey itself. When we see them as obstacles that God should have protected us from, we are inclined to reason that all our prayers for protection do not work. Since our prayers arise from our faith, we conclude in our frustration that faith does not work.

At this present moment, I seem to be standing at the bottom of a very deep bomb crater, unable and powerless to get out. It leaves me wondering whether this explosion is going to mark the very end of my journey.

The Bible teaches me that God *always* works; therefore, faith *always* works because God *always* works. If this is so, then God, who is always faithful to Himself, must always supply what our faith needs.

Faith does not work by God doing everything I ask Him to do, as though He owes me something or needs to prove Himself. The truth is, God owes me nothing, and I owe Him everything. Even when a bomb hits, His word to me inspires and reassures me that His grace is sufficient for me. The only reason I survived my Desert Place was because the word of God sustained me and pulled me out of that particular earth-shattering explosion. That same word is doing the same thing today. I do not need God to prove Himself by healing me. He has already proved Himself at the cross by healing me of the most destructive disease ever: the spiritual disease of sin. As I stand in the depth of my deep crater, unable to see over the steep sides of the crater wall, I know that God will supply what my faith needs. For that, all I need to focus upon is the finished work of Jesus at the cross.

Faith Feeds on God's Word

God has chosen to use the Bible as the source through which He reveals Himself and His purposes. Studying the Bible is the primary way in which God speaks into our lives and feeds our faith. Through studying the Bible, we learn what faith is and what it is not. It was my study of the Bible in my Desert Place which sustained me and brought me into such tremendous revelation and hope. I do not claim that my study of the Bible has led me to become an expert theologian who has all the answers, but what I do claim is that studying the Bible prepares me not to be surprised by the unexpected. Whatever else the Bible reveals to us, its main thrust is to lead us into a knowledge of who God is and the good news of His salvation plan that finds fulfilment only in Jesus. Without the knowledge of this salvation, the Bible is just a very old history book.

Biblical Illiteracy

The Bible is God's written word to us, so why do so many Christians today have such little time and interest in what God has to say to us in its pages? Why do so many Christians neglect it? Before my Desert Place, I was one such Christian, so I can answer that question first-hand. I never saw the real need to study it; after all, I was already a Christian, so surely it was not really necessary for me to give it much time. I did think that it was probably a good thing to read, yet at the same time, I believed it was something that I could take or leave. I was content to listen to the Sunday sermon at church and leave the serious study of the Bible to the so-called experts. As long as I felt that they were not saying something terribly off-hand or heretical, I was content to take on board whatever they said and leave it at that. I was happy to rely on others to spoon-feed me bits of the Bible, but in doing so, I was not learning to feed for myself. Even though I had considered myself to be a Christian for so many years, my biblical illiteracy and ignorance starved me of spiritual food, and I remained an infant in Christ at best.

Possessing the knowledge of Scripture goes hand in hand with understanding the character of God and acquiring the mind of Christ. Having a thorough knowledge of Scripture leads to a correct understanding of what Christ has saved us *from*, and what He has saved us *for.* One of the biggest dangers of biblical illiteracy is that it leads to a distinct lack of spiritual insight and discernment. Any church can be full of decent, good, nice people who display some form of intellectual assertion to the very basics of Christianity, yet they are powerless to reflect the life of Christ and the assurance of salvation simply because of biblical illiteracy.

A healthy faith is a strong faith that feeds on healthy spiritual food. That healthy food is the whole counsel of God as written in the Bible and feeds on its truth. A healthy faith needs a regular diet that provides wholesome, nutritional, spiritual food that builds up our spiritual immune system to protect us from false spirits, while strengthening the muscles of faith that need to be exercised. Biblical illiteracy is akin to going on hunger strike, resulting in a weak faith that lacks an appetite for the truth of God's word. This, in turn, makes us vulnerable to spiritual sickness and deception and a sure sign that all is not well with our spiritual well-being.

Christians need to know the Bible for themselves. Sadly, the Bible is one of the most abused books on the planet, especially by those who profess to be religious, spiritual or Christian. Selected Scriptures are ripped out of their proper context to get them to mean something they were never intended to mean. In this way, the Bible is misinterpreted so that it suits our purposes and agendas, leading to all kinds of false teaching and acceptance of error. We embrace the bits that we agree with and disregard the rest as irrelevant and out of date. A weakness that plagues a lot of younger Christians is that, rather than bringing themselves to the Bible, they prefer the convenience of turning on Christian TV and let the popular, motivational speakers feed them with what they want to hear.

The problem is that many of these teachers do not tell us the whole truth. They keep us tuned in by telling us that God loves us so much and that He wants to bless us with worldly success and happiness. We love this kind of stuff since it demands nothing from us but promises us everything. People use Christian media not only as an excuse to neglect their Bible but an excuse to neglect their local church. In this way, Christians are robbing their local church of their presence and witness.

We do not study the Bible only to fill up our heads with knowledge. It is possible to be the world's most knowledgeable theologian yet still have no saving faith. Without doubt, the truth of God's word must first speak into our minds, but from there, it must transform us from the inside out. Allowing God to speak His word into our lives is not just an academic exercise but a spiritual workout. Feeding on God's word, together with prayer, forms an integral part of the expression of our dependency upon God. Through the study of the Bible, God's word comes to life within us as we digest its contents and allow the Holy Spirit to help us understand what we read and apply it to our lives. To know God's word in this way provides us with a spiritual fuel that energizes us to live out a real faith.

I cannot emphasize enough the impact that God's written word had upon me in my Desert Place. It shook me out of my spiritual complacency and opened my eyes to see how spiritually bankrupt I actually was. Here's the thing; I would not have recognized my spiritual shallowness unless I had taken myself to the Scriptures. They both sustained me and taught me many important lessons, which continue to speak to me just as much today as they did back then. Till the day of our death, we can never exhaust ourselves of what the Bible has to teach us.

Chapter 7

FAITH DOES SO MUCH MORE

Faith Sees the Hand of God

God has used the whole of my life to shape and develop my faith. It is a faith that begins at the cross and grows from that place of death, repentance, forgiveness, justification and resurrection to a new life. It is a new life of a faith that saves, and lives this life trusting in Jesus.

With eyes of faith, I can look back over my life and discern the hand of God's activity. I find it easier to verify His activity by looking back rather than trying to establish where He is in the present. The sceptic might say that I am reading God back into what has already taken place. For sure, faith does not live in the past; it is active in the present and always looks forward. Yet faith is strengthened as we look back and are able to detect the hand of God's leading and provision. Through all that has taken place in the past, I can see how God has been at work in my life as He has rescued, led, guided and provided for me. With eyes of faith, I recognize His hand in my past, supplying me with the confidence to know that His hand is at work in the whole of my future. Faith allows me to live in a state of complete trust and a determined submission to the Lordship of Jesus over my life, body and soul. Faith allows me to understand from Scripture that I have been chosen and called according to God's will and purposes.

'And we know that for those who love God all things work together for good, for those who are called according to his purpose. For those whom he foreknew he also predestined to be conformed to the image of his Son, in order that he might be the firstborn among many brothers. And those

whom he predestined he also called, and those whom he called he also justified, and those whom he justified he also glorified. What then shall we say to these things? If God is for us, who can be against us?' (Rom. 8:28–31).

Faith empowers me to see the bigger picture: past, present and future. Whether in my own life or the wider context of the whole of human history, I see God bringing to completion all that He intends to do.

Faith Produces Good Fruit

'For as the body apart from the spirit is dead, so also faith apart from works is dead' (James 2:26).

Authentic faith always produces good fruit; it cannot produce bad fruit or even no fruit at all. To live without faith in Jesus is synonymous to living in sin, yet the unregenerate person recognizes none of this because they are blinded to their true spiritual condition. The same can be said for the person who appears to be spiritual yet who produce bad fruit. Jesus once said:

'Beware of false prophets, who come to you in sheep's clothing but inwardly are ravenous wolves. You will recognize them by their fruits. Are grapes gathered from thorn bushes, or figs from thistles? So, every healthy tree bears good fruit, but the diseased tree bears bad fruit. A healthy tree cannot bear bad fruit, nor can a diseased tree bear good fruit. Every tree that does not bear good fruit is cut down and thrown into the fire. Thus you will recognize them by their fruits' (Matt.7:15–20).

The Bible teaches us that anything that is not of faith is sin (Heb.11:6). We do not have to possess faith in order to produce good fruit, such as doing good, being kind, charitable and helpful. We do not need to have faith in order to be a nice person or have admirable qualities about our personality and character. But if these things do not come out of obedience and love for God, it is sin because we do it all independently of God and not for His glory. Faith never sets out to do wrong or bad, rather, the bad fruit we produce reveals the absence of faith and the presence of sin. Jesus said:

> *'Abide in me, and I in you. As the branch cannot bear fruit by itself, unless it abides in the vine, neither can you, unless you abide in me. I am the vine; you are the branches. Whoever abides in me and I in him, he it is that bears much fruit, for apart from me you can do nothing'* (John 15:4–5).

> *'I am the true vine, and my Father is the vinedresser. Every branch in me that does not bear fruit, he takes away, and every branch that does bear fruit he prunes, that it may bear more fruit'* (John 15:1–2).

The Apostle Paul writes about the fruit of the Holy Spirit who indwells every true believer:

> *'But the fruit of the Spirit is love, joy, peace, patience, kindness, goodness, faithfulness, gentleness and self-control'* (Gal.5:22–23).

As the Holy Spirit abides in the person of faith, He grows the fruit of His presence within them which results in a life lived in love for God and one another.

Faith Transforms a Person's Life

In this way, the Holy Spirit changes a person from the inside out, transforming a person's mind and will. This is the work of God that brings to life a spiritual renewal that accompanies genuine faith.

Some Christians live as though they only want heaven because they do not want hell. Their only incentive to get into heaven is simply to escape hell. I dare say that is how many people have started out on their Christian journey, yet true faith will soon move us forward from that starting point. True faith never stands still and always moves forwards. If our faith is real, it will compel us to press on towards our heavenly calling as the Spirit within us creates a deep desire to *want* to know and understand more of God, together with a heartfelt desire to do His will.

A person of faith or, to put it another way, a faithful person, can look forward to a place in heaven when they die. Such a person already belongs in the kingdom of God in the here and now. While we still live in this fallen world and these fallen bodies, the presence of God's kingdom is made available to us but in a veiled way. When the time comes for our earthly bodies to pass away, our spirit will be ushered into the fullness of God's unveiled presence in heaven. If someone is only interested in getting into heaven to avoid hell, they will have no interest in living in the kingdom and presence of God now. Furthermore, they will see no need to build up their faith since they believe that they already have their ticket to heaven. While there is no entrance fee into heaven, living in the kingdom of God in the present will cost you everything. Are you prepared to lay down your life, follow Jesus and pay that cost? If not, then the Bible questions the validity of your faith.

The validity of our faith will be proven by the good fruit that we produce. Jesus told a parable that went like this:

> *'A sower went out to sow. As he sowed, some seeds fell along the path, and the birds came and devoured them. Other seeds fell on rocky ground, where they did not have much soil, and immediately they sprang up, since they had no depth of soil. But when the sun rose they were scorched. And since they had no root, they withered away. Other seeds fell among thorns, and the thorns grew up and choked them. Other seeds fell on good soil and produced*

grain, some a hundredfold, some sixty, some thirty. He who has ears, let him hear' (Matt. 13:3–9).

Jesus then explained the parable to His followers:

'Hear then the parable of the sower: When anyone hears the word of the kingdom and does not understand it, the evil one comes and snatches away what has been sown in his heart. This is what was sown along the path. As for what was sown on rocky ground, this is the one who hears the word and immediately receives it with joy, yet he has no root in himself, but endures for a while, and when tribulation or persecution arises on account of the word, immediately he falls away. As for what was sown among the thorns, this is the one who hears the word, but the cares of this world and the deceitfulness of riches choke the word, and it proves unfruitful. As for what was sown on good soil, this is the one who hears the word and understands it. He indeed bears fruit and yields, in one case a hundredfold, in another sixty, and in another thirty.' (Matt. 13:18–23).

This parable tells us about four different types of soil that represent four different people who hear the word of God and the message of salvation. The one who proclaims that word (the sower) is not the point of the parable. The point of the parable is the condition of the soil. The seed that the sower sows (which is God's word of salvation) is always the same. Out of these four people who hear God's word, only one is truly affected by the word so that an authentic faith is produced. The first person hears the word but does not understand with their mind; the word does not sink in or have any impact and is quickly removed. The second person understands well enough, so that the gospel message of salvation initially fills them with joy, but when they begin to understand what it will cost to follow Jesus, they abandon the gospel and go back to their former ways. The third person understands with their mind but whatever faith is born remains shallow and superficial. It proves to be of no effect, unable to stand up to the reality of life's temptations and trials. For them, God has not turned out to be the God they wanted him to be. The fourth person hears and understands, so that the word penetrates deeply, giving rise to a faith that goes on to transform their lives, the evidence of which is to produce Godly fruit which can be clearly seen and lasts. This last person represents soil that has been prepared to receive the seed of God's word and develops a deep-rooted love and commitment to follow Jesus.

The starting point of faith is where the seed takes root in well-prepared soil. Our starting point may well be a motivation to gain a place in heaven in order to avoid hell, but a starting point it must remain. If our faith does not begin to grow, mature and deepen, it will not become the faith that Jesus said we need in order to follow Him and be saved. From the three passages above, we see that faith does not love the world but overcomes it. This is a sure sign of authentic faith and one whose whole outlook on life in this world has undergone a radical, supernatural transformation that reflects a deep-rooted love for Christ. The Apostle John wrote:

> *'For everyone who has been born of God overcomes the world. And this is the victory that has overcome the world— our faith. Who is it that overcomes the world except the one who believes that Jesus is the Son of God?'* (1 John 5:4–5).

Real Faith Prays Real Prayers

When you pray, where do your prayers come from? Do you talk *at* God as though you are merely *saying* your prayers to Him? Do your prayers come only from your head? Is your praying a matter of routine or recital? Do you pray from a wish list, placing your orders before God? When you pray in public, do you put on your respectable prayer voice and pray polite prayers? Where our prayers come from is hugely significant, since it affects *how* we pray and *what* we pray, revealing a lot about our faith. A real faith prays real prayers that come not only from the head but also from the heart.

Real prayers are prayed from a real faith that lives in the real world. Real prayer is simply the demonstration of our total dependency upon God. Real prayer is not a casual communication that is produced by a half-hearted affiliation with God; real prayer flows from a deep-rooted devotion that connects us with God. This is the kind of prayer that knows what it means to cry out to God. I would say that if you have never prayed with tears, you have never really known what it means to pray. Real prayers often struggle to find adequate and sufficient words as we bring ourselves to God. Since we live in a fallen world, in fallen bodies, surrounded by the presence of sin and its evil consequences, our prayers become a constant daily necessity as we live in the frustration and desperation of a fallen world. Real prayers require our honesty, humility and dependency upon God.

Faith Lives in Obedience to God

Faith is the expression of obedience, not out of duty, but from a heart and mind that desires to love God because of who He is. It works from a longing to live for the glory of God in all that we do, say and even think. Whatever we do that does not glorify God is not an outworking of faith. The Apostle Paul wrote:

'Whatever does not proceed from faith is sin' (Rom.14:23).

We see the evidence that our faith is alive and functioning when we make it our goal to live in obedience to the first commandment. Jesus said that the first and greatest commandment is to:

'Love the Lord your God with all your heart and with all your soul and with all your mind' (Matt. 22:37).

Jesus also said that if we love Him, we *will* obey His commandments (John 15:10). This is not a 'might' obey, but a 'will' obey, a wilful obedience that is driven to do the will and purposes of God. If we deliberately choose not to obey, the Spirit will convict us of our sin so that we recognize it and lead us to repentance and back to the place of obedience. Loving God is not a sentimental, romantic thing by which our love for God is based on our feelings and emotions. Neither is it a legalistic ticking-the-box exercise of obeying rules. Rather, our love for God is a response that emanates from a true understanding of God's love for us, so clearly demonstrated at the cross.

Paul writes in Romans 1:5 about '*the obedience of faith.*' This obedience is to '*work out your own salvation*' that Paul mentions in Philippians 2:12.

Before finding myself in my Desert Place, I was proactive in the life of the church and held to Christian principles and practices, yet I did not truly love God. Ironically, it was the severity of the Desert Place that taught me what it actually meant to love God. It was there that God brought me into a far greater appreciation and understanding of how astonishingly great is the love of God for me, demonstrated so powerfully at the cross. God went that far and to that length to reveal His love. The cross manifests the sufficiency of God's grace *over* me, together with the sufficiency of God's love *for* me. These two things go hand in hand. Too many Christians do not love God very much because they have not grasped the immensity of God's love for them. We can only give what we are willing to receive. Such an understanding of God's love for us is very powerful, leading to a rock-solid resolution of the heart and mind to express our love for Him in return by living in obedience to Him. Like the love of Christ expressed at the cross, it is a sacrificial love that is prepared to count the cost, whatever that might be. Obedience flows from the person who knows that they are loved by God. He loves us not because He is forced to, but because He chose to and wants to. So too, we obey God not because we have to, but because we want to.

Faith in this Life Invests in the Next

The Apostle James writes:

'Come now, you who say, "Today or tomorrow we will go into such and such a town and spend a year there and trade and make a profit"— yet you do not know what tomorrow will bring. What is your life? For you are a mist that appears for a little time and then vanishes' (James 4:13–14).

This life is just a blip, whereas the next life is where we will get to spend the whole of eternity. This life is a rehearsal and preparation for the next. This life sets the scene for the next, determining what rewards (responsibilities) we will receive in the next, depending upon how we have served God in this life. This has got nothing to do with our salvation, for salvation is a gift of God's grace and mercy. However, while it is our faith in Jesus that saves us for the next life, that same faith will manifest itself in this life as we do good works. Jesus taught that God will reward the good that we do, even when it is done in secret:

'Beware of practicing your righteousness before other people in order to be seen by them, for then you will have no reward from your Father who is in heaven. Thus, when you give to the needy, sound no trumpet before you, as the hypocrites do in the synagogues and in the streets, that they may be praised by others. Truly, I say to you, they have received their reward. But when you give to the needy, do not let your left hand know what your right hand is doing, so that your giving may be in secret. And the Father who sees in secret will reward you. And when you pray, you must not be like the hypocrites. For they love to stand and pray in the synagogues and at the street corners, that they may be seen by others. Truly, I say to you, they have received their reward. But when you pray, go into your room and shut the door and pray to your Father who is in secret. And your Father who sees in secret will reward you' (Matt. 6:1–6).

Chapter 8

TRUE FAITH LIVES

Authentic faith is alive and active. It breathes and moves as the Holy Spirit lives in us and through us. Faith is not something we switch on when we have our religious moments and then switch off when we no longer need it. Faith is a way of life, which means it cannot be hidden or go unnoticed. Real faith lives as we live; the two go together (James 2:14–26).

Faith is Personal

My faith will not get you into heaven, and neither will your faith get me into heaven. I cannot give you my faith, and you cannot give me yours. Faith cannot be passed on from parent to child as something to be inherited. Neither can anyone bestow faith upon a baby at a christening ceremony. Faith is extremely personal, encompassing the mind, body and soul of the individual. When the time comes, we will personally stand before Jesus to give an account of our life. You and I will not stand with our church, friends or family. This will be a one-on-one encounter where our faith will be examined.

Faith Does Not Hide

While faith is extremely personal, it does not hide away or keep silent. Faith is not a private arrangement that we have with God. Real faith is visible so that we can see its effect. If we cannot see or hear it in the way we live and talk, it is not real faith. True faith lives as a testimony to the salvation and good news that Jesus has brought us into. It is lived out in the real world as a light that shines in the darkness.

Faith must live or else it is not real faith. Faith only becomes a reality when it is firmly embedded in life itself. I believe in a Jesus who was raised bodily back to life after His crucifixion and who now lives in heaven. My faith lives in Him because He is alive, and by His Spirit, He lives in me. When faith is born, it is brought to life and energized by the Holy Spirit. What God has birthed in me is not some kind of psychological, philosophical or intellectual obsession; it is a spiritual phenomenon. At present, Jesus remains bodily in heaven until it is time for Him to return to the earth. In the meantime, the Holy Spirit dwells in me as the replacement or standby, providing me with comfort, help and support (John 14:16–26).

If someone says to me that they have a faith, I expect to see proof of that faith by the way they apply it to the reality of life. A faith that is only brought out when it suits or on Sunday mornings is a part-time, superficial faith. It is a dead faith because it does not live in daily communion with Jesus. Jesus is not a Sunday person, He is a way of life; He is the way, the truth and the life (John 14:6).

I have never liked plastic flowers no matter how beautiful and realistic they appear. While they might look good, I know they are not authentic. They can look so much like the real thing, and sometimes I have to feel them to convince myself they are not real. I don't like them because they pretend to be something they are not, posing as a mere substitute for the real thing. The missing ingredient is that there is no life in them whatsoever. The beauty of an authentic flower is the way it presents itself as something that has grown and blossomed into something so colourful and intricate. The same cannot be said of a plastic faith that possesses nothing more than a cosmetic make-over. This artificial faith is not from God, and He cannot do anything with it since it holds no intrinsic value and will never stand up to the time of testing. A dead faith remains powerless and ineffective, especially when times get tough.

Faith is a gift from God and since it is from Him, He is certain to test it. The testing does not test to see how well God is doing but how we respond to the faith He has given to us. Since faith does not hide away, the testing of faith is very often put on public display for all to see. This forms a key part to the public witness of our faith, revealing the depth of trust and confidence that we have in the sufficiency of Jesus, especially under difficult circumstances.

True Faith Grows as it Lives

We do not suddenly wake up one morning and have faith. The Bible teaches that faith comes through hearing the gospel message of Jesus Christ spoken to the mind through which we can understand and respond (Rom. 10:17). Faith is not just a possession of the knowledge of salvation, although without that knowledge, we can never possess a faith that saves. Faith is not a method, formula, ritual or something we achieve from reading a textbook or passing a theological exam. From these things, we can learn what faith is, but faith in itself is not learned, it is applied. We learn to apply and live out faith as we continue to place our faith in Jesus within the reality of everyday life. It does not matter how many master's degrees in theology one has, courses completed, or seminars attended, faith cannot be awarded or earned. The knowledge of salvation leads to a faith that is proven in the real world, where nothing is staged, programmed or set up. Because the world is all messed up and unpredictable, applying faith is not neat and tidy but messy and sometimes confusing.

Faith Needs to be Fed with Truth

Learning biblical theology and doctrine are key essentials to a growing faith. Faith needs to be informed by our knowledge and understanding of the biblical doctrines. Theology and doctrine are spiritual truths that keep our faith on the straight and narrow way. They serve to support and nurture our faith as they provide us with the bigger picture of the greatness of who God is, what He has done and what He will yet do. Too many churches and Christians have little desire for theology or doctrine, considering them to be stuffy, legalistic, rule-driven and non-essential. Ignoring these spiritual essentials and starving ourselves of their truths leads to a dangerous ignorance that is deprived of an understanding of what a real faith is and what it looks like. Many Christians have a bad theology or no theology at all. This creates a vacuum in which people make up their own pragmatic theology that feels right for them and makes them happy, a happiness that has more to do with human feelings and the pleasing of self rather than pleasing God.

Faith is Vision

The world you and I live in demands our constant attention. It says, 'look at me' and has a seductive and persuasive pull that draws us into coveting what it has to offer. This is precisely what today's marketing and advertising industry seeks to achieve. It is a strategy that seeks to tempt us with something new, sowing a seed of dissatisfaction with what we already have. To covet means to long for something or desire to have what we do not already have. We covet first with our eyes, focusing on what we desire and feed our minds with a vision of how much happier life would be if only we had those things. The truth is, no matter how much we have, we never quite have enough, and the novelty of our new acquisition soon wears off and we want something new. This kind of vision has a gaze that is fixed upon worldly things, which can never truly satisfy because they never last. Biblical faith has a vision that gazes upon heavenly things that have a lasting, eternal value.

'Set your minds on things that are above, not on the things that are on the earth' (Col. 3:2).

'Do not love the world or the things in the world. If anyone loves the world, the love of the Father is not in him. For all

that is in the world—the desires of the flesh and the desires of the eyes and pride of life is not from the Father but is from the world. And the world is passing away along with its desires, but whoever does the will of God abides forever' (1 John 2:15–17).

'Do not lay up for yourselves treasures on earth, where moth and rust destroy and where thieves break in and steal, but lay up for yourselves treasures in heaven, where neither moth nor rust destroys and where thieves do not break in and steal. For where your treasure is, there your heart will be also' (Matt. 6:19–21).

As a follower of Jesus Christ, I am determined to resist anyone or anything that has the potential to cloud my vision of him. I am convinced that Jesus is everything I really need because only He can provide me with the satisfaction of eternal salvation. He is my life, hope and future. Faith has big eyes that see a bigger vision which looks beyond this life. It is a vision that is focused upon Jesus and centred on an eternal future with Him in His kingdom, whereas the alternative is to hold to a vision that is fixed on what this world has to offer, which can never last and is destined to pass away.

Every morning I wake up on death row as a condemned cancer victim. There are so many other people who wake up facing the same fate as I do. Just like me, these fellow sufferers know that there is nothing they can do to heal themselves. I dare say that some think they might stand a chance by changing their diet or something else. I dare say that many of my fellow sufferers are resigned to putting up a brave fight till the very last breath. Others might resolve to be stoic about life and death, holding to a philosophical view of 'whatever will be will be,' or, 'everything happens for a reason'. I dare say that most of my fellow sufferers will demonstrate a degree of inspirational courage, choosing to look away from the negatives to focus on all of the positives they have had in life. Along with me, they no doubt recognize that they have not been singled out as the only human being ever to have faced death, comforting themselves with the solid fact that sooner or later, everyone is condemned to die of something.

When anyone is diagnosed with a terminal illness, all hope of life disappears because the end is in sight, yet it need not be this way. As someone who has faith, my vision looks beyond death's doors, and I can face the death of my body knowing that I still have a future hope. This hope and vision provide me with the confidence and courage which sustains me in my present predicament. My faith does not rest on my personal ability to become some kind of a superhero who battles with cancer to see how long I can last. Instead, my faith relies upon my vision of Jesus, through whom I see the bigger picture of how the whole story ends. The Christian sees their death as something that gives rise to a glorious new beginning.

Walk by Faith and Not by Sight

Our life is like a journey, having a beginning, end and everything in between. As a Christ follower, I aim to travel this journey full of a faith that Christ will walk this journey with me. When my journey comes to an end, and I can walk no more, I have the faith to believe that Jesus will carry me on to be with Him in heaven. Since I cannot visibly see Jesus with my eyes, I have to walk by faith and not by sight. This is not an easy thing to do since I live in a world where everything that matters is visual.

'Now faith is the assurance of things hoped for, the conviction of things not seen' (Heb. 11:1).

I listen to the prayers of people who pray for the church, asking God to show us the way forward and to make His plans known to us. While I understand such an approach, those prayers make it sound as though the way forward and God's plans are a hidden mystery yet to be revealed. Bear in mind, God has already told us everything we need to know in the Bible. Even so, our prayers often reflect a reliance on wanting everything to be mapped out, programmed and planned, reducing faith to something that can be visibly presented to the church. Instead, we ought to pray for God to do what He needs to do in each one of us as we surrender in full obedience to what He has already asked of us in His word. His word is the word of faith, and we must be full of His word if we are to be faithful to His word.

Faith Sees the Bigger Picture

Faith in Jesus enables us to see the bigger picture. Through faith, we see the miracle of Jesus's birth, followed about 33 years later by the miracle of His resurrection after His death. The resurrection tells me that God had a clear purpose in it all. In spite of the way things looked, the resurrection proves that God ordained and was in control of the crucifixion all along. In His physical death, Jesus identified Himself with my death, and through His bodily resurrection, I can identify myself with that same resurrection and the renewed body that will one day be mine. This bigger picture tells me that, in spite of the way things look now, God has not abandoned me. I find rest in the resurrection, ascension, and glorification of Jesus through which I, too, will be raised and glorified with a redeemed body made fit to dwell in God's eternal kingdom.

One Day at a Time

In the meantime, I live in the here and the now, one day at a time. As I look at the day ahead, I recognize that this day has been granted to me by God. What is the point of today? The point of today is to honour and glorify God, bearing witness to the sufficiency of His grace and the salvation I have in Jesus. Today, I will take refuge in Jesus, for in Him I see the goodness, mercy and love of God. Speaking of Jesus, Hebrews 1:3 tells us: *'He is the radiance of his glory and the exact imprint of his nature.'*

I am incredibly blessed that I can always take refuge in Jesus, both in life and death.

My illness is not a failure of faith or an accident made by God. While I do not claim to understand it all, God has given to me an opportunity through my illness to testify to the salvation I have in Jesus in a more effective way than I could when I was fit and well. I have been given the opportunity to bear witness to the fact that, while I still live in a fallen body, this life is not all there is. I do not put my hope or trust in this life since it is all temporary and passing away. My witness is that Jesus is my life, both now and in the future. Death will simply release me into the fullness of His glorious presence.

Faith Always Trusts

If God can do anything He so desires, why has He allowed cancer to invade my body? Why has He allowed the frustrating side effect of ocular myasthenia gravis to take hold of my eyes and thus bring the original immunotherapy treatment to an abrupt end? Why has God withheld a successful outcome from the treatment I have had to correct my eyes, which in turn, would have resulted in the restart of immunotherapy? Why does God allow the many prayers for my healing to go unanswered? Who will answer these questions for me?

The Bible teaches me that God is *always* trustworthy. What does that mean? How am I expected to trust in a God who has allowed cancer to condemn me to death?

Unlike us, God cannot lie or do evil. He is always faithful to His word and that makes Him trustworthy. If God is always trustworthy, then I can trust in Him no matter what. Trust enables me to believe that He is in overall control in every situation. Trust believes that God has the power and authority to step in to intervene in any situation and at any time if He so chooses. Equally, God has the power and authority not to step in and intervene. Many prayers have been offered up to God asking for my healing, yet these prayers remain unanswered. Nevertheless, because I trust in the word of God, my unanswered prayers do not prevent me from trusting in Him, no matter what my feelings might tell me.

Faith is Trust and Brings Perfect Peace

Does faith in God mean I will live a peaceful life? No. Faith takes God at His word. Isaiah wrote:

> *'You keep him in perfect peace whose mind is stayed on you because he trusts in you'* (Isa. 26:3).

This is a verse that I have found particularly challenging throughout my ministry but especially during my illness. It speaks not just of peace but *perfect* peace. How on earth can I have perfect peace in my situation and be kept there all the time? Jesus told His disciples:

> *'Peace I leave with you; my peace I give to you. Not as the world gives do I give to you. Let not your hearts be troubled, neither let them be afraid'* (John 14:27).

Both of the above verses speak of the same perfect peace. Only God can provide this perfect peace. It is a supernatural peace that comes from a supernatural source. It is a peace that a fallen world cannot provide or replicate. In my current place of testing, I am desperate to possess the perfect peace that only God can provide.

What comes to mind right now are the biblical stories where God's people suffered terrible persecution. For example, consider some of the Old Testament characters, such as Daniel, who was thrown alive to the lions because he defied the king's edict by continuing to pray to Yahweh, the God of Israel (Daniel 6). Then there are Shadrach, Meshach, and Abednego, who refused to be unfaithful to God by worshipping the golden image that King

70

Nebuchadnezzar had set up. These men were prepared to face the consequences and were thrown alive into the fiery furnace (Daniel 3). It would seem that all these men were prepared and ready to face up to their cruel demise, not by panicking but by feeding on the peace of God given to them at that time. In both these stories, God protected the victims from *within* their trial and completely delivered them out of their trial. During the severity of their trial, they possessed a peace that equipped them to stand firm in the Lord their God, whatever the outcome. The Apostle Paul writes:

'Do not be anxious about anything, but in everything by prayer and supplication with thanksgiving let your requests be made known to God. And the peace of God, which surpasses all understanding, will guard your hearts and your mind in Christ Jesus' (Phil. 4:6–7).

Does God expect me to be super-human? Most certainly not! Neither do I want the added pressure of attempting to come across as being such a person. The peace that God makes available is not to be at peace with my pain but to be at peace with God. It is a perfect peace because God is perfect. He is perfect in His faithfulness to save me for Himself, which He has already done. My perfect peace is found in a perfect God who will never leave me nor forsake me. My perfect peace is given to me as I focus on who God is and not my circumstances or grief. The trustworthiness of God *must* exceed the very worst possible scenario, or else He is not trustworthy at all. My faith in Jesus empowers me to trust God completely and without conditions attached. That does not make me super-human, but it does reflect a supernatural peace and confidence that is given by God to those whose faith is placed completely in His trustworthiness.

The Bible teaches me that I can trust in God at all times. I can always trust because God is always consistent within Himself and His character. This means that I trust not only in what He does but in what He does not do. God is *always* faithful to His promises and to the salvation He has given to me in Jesus. In contradiction to the way things appear, God is *always* working for my good; therefore, how can I *not* trust in Him? It is this trust that keeps me in *perfect* peace. There is a constant daily perseverance taking place in my life, in which I fight to maintain this peace by continuing to look to God through Jesus, taking refuge in Him.

Faith that Finds Rest

The Bible tells me at least 66 times that God is sovereign, which means that I can believe that He is in total control of my illness. That assurance opens up for me a whole lot of rest and peace. I can find rest in God's sovereignty, knowing that He only does what is right and never does wrong. I can find rest, trusting that Jesus is not only Lord of all, but Lord of my whole body, life and soul. That means that I can trust Him, come what may. I can happily make the positive confession that Jesus is in charge of my life, and I am satisfied in surrendering my life to Him. I can also make the positive confession that Satan has no power or authority over me because I belong to Christ, and therefore, I come under the absolute power and authority of Christ. I have already been delivered from the dominion of Satan and transferred into the kingdom of God's Son. That speaks of my assured salvation and who I belong to and where I am heading! Not only does the Bible tell me that God is sovereign, it also tells me at least 73 times that God is eternal. If my trust in God was only for this life, then what is there to be gained in that?

> '*If in Christ we have hope in this life only, we are of all people most to be pitied*' (1 Cor. 15:19).

I can only make sense of finding rest in God's sovereignty as I look beyond this life, towards what is stored up for me in heaven and in the age to come.

Chapter 9

FAITH AND FEELINGS

In the early days of my Desert Place, I remember my dad trying his best to encourage me by reminding me of a particular Bible verse that I have already mentioned:

'And we know that for those who love God all things work together for good, for those who are called according to his purpose' (Rom. 8:28).

I also remember thinking that even if that were true, it certainly didn't look or feel that way.

In the latter days of my Desert Place, I grew to understand that my faith in Jesus must never be driven by my feelings. To have faith in Jesus is to have a clear vision of Jesus. It is a vision that looks to Jesus and the truth that He is. Nothing passes as truth because it *feels* like the truth; it is either true or it is not. If you were to ask me right now, 'Do you *feel* that God loves you?' I would have to answer, no. If my faith relied on my feelings, I would have abandoned my faith many years ago. Yet, by the grace of God, I know who Jesus is and that He loves me. How do I know He loves me? I only have to look at the cross to see the greatest demonstration of love for me that anyone could ever express. My feelings are temporal and can be changed by my mood swings and even by the weather! If my faith is to be effective and enduring, it must be built on nothing less than the solid rock of Jesus and the salvation I have in Him.

From time to time, people have asked me how I am feeling. It is a natural question to ask. However, I am pierced with terminal cancers that have no other agenda apart from killing me off. In addition, my eye defects are extremely frustrating to live with and are a burden to my ministry. These are things I can never feel good about, no matter how much the sun is shining and the birds are singing.

While my feelings and emotions are an integral part of being human, they are untrustworthy and wholly unreliable. They can so easily lead me down the path of confusion, doubt, insecurity and self-pity. My feelings fuel my sense of hopelessness and despair. I know that I am in good company with the Psalmists of the Bible, who were honest enough to reveal the reality of their own struggles in regard to their innermost human emotions and feelings.

When a kind, well-meaning person asks me how I am feeling, I do not think that they really want me to give them the honest full-blown exposition of how rotten I sometimes feel. As a man of faith, I know that my daily battle is not to allow my feelings to drive or govern my faith. My feelings set out to weaken my faith, but I know that my faith in God builds me up and encourages me. My faith tells me that my Sovereign God is always reliable and in control, even when my feelings would like to dictate otherwise.

I am made up of a soul and body. If someone were to ask me how my body is, I could tell them that my body is not at all well. But if someone were to ask me how my soul is, which is the essence of my person and the real me who has been redeemed by Christ, I can confidently tell them that my soul is well and couldn't be better. This shifts the focus away from my feelings and body onto what really matters; the condition of my soul which always lives in the joy of my salvation.

Since my feelings and emotions are extremely real because I am a real human being, it is necessary that I possess a faith that is even more real. One of the most important things I have had to train myself to do each day is to feed my faith and not my feelings. I feed my faith by focusing on Jesus, who is the author and perfecter of my faith. I know that in Him I am safe and secure, even when it does not feel like it.

Sometimes, when I am feeling weak and fuzzy in the head, I feel fed up, *really* fed up. I feel flat, demotivated and that I have had enough. This is further fuelled by my tiredness and droopy eyes. What is more, I am tired of living in a world in which God remains hidden and silent. I am tired of not hearing Him with my ears and seeing Him with my eyes. At times such as this, I have moments when I question why faith has to be so difficult. I question why God does not empower every person who has a true faith to experience a more tangible awareness of His presence within them. My greatest need every day is to know that the presence of God is with me, yet when I get fed up, it feels as though the presence of God is so very far away.

Not only do I feel fed up because God remains hidden from sight, I am also tired of living in a fallen, broken world. I am fed up with being surrounded by the presence of sin, together with its evil consequences of suffering and injustice. I am fed up living in a world whose god is the Devil. None of this makes me feel good or happy but, in my frustration, I remind myself that I do not belong to this fallen world and that I am no more of this world than Jesus is (John 17:16). The presence of the power of sin and death means that nothing is normal, at least not in the way God originally intended. When I consider the perfection of God's original creation, I realize how abnormal life in this world really is. I am constantly reminded of this by the condemnation of my physical predicament, yet the truth is that these things are normal in a fallen world, which is why we need hospitals and doctors!

In my frustration, I often feel spiritually lonely and isolated. These moments send me to God in prayer since I have nowhere else to go and no one else to confide in. God is the only one who I can offload my burdens onto, knowing that He will understand because He knows all things and is my refuge. Sometimes I have no more prayers left in me since I have run out of words. At such times, I simply bring myself to God in silence, as though I can do no more but wait upon Him and weep, knowing that my weeping is an expression of my crying out to God. It is a cry which He surely understands so much more than I do.

My greatest daily need is to know that the presence of God *is* with me and that I am *not* alone. Does this mean that my faith is inadequate or insufficient? I do not believe so, since my longing to know the presence of God reveals the authenticity of my faith, a longing that will only be satisfied on the day of my death or the return of Jesus Christ.

I long for others to live in His presence, but it seems to me that many Christians today are not so keen to leave this world. Their desire is to stay here and have their best life now, which I think reflects a greater love for the things of this world rather than a longing to be living in the presence and glory of God.

Chapter 10

DOES FAITH HEAL?

I have been given books that tell the stories of terminally ill Christians healing themselves. They have healed themselves by 'naming and claiming' their healing through speaking and confessing certain Scriptures. Such stories, which are difficult to verify, add an additional strain and burden to my already existing burden of illness. Since God has not healed me of His own accord, it would suggest that the only way for me to gain my healing is through the self-effort of naming and claiming my healing. This teaching lies at the very heart of the Word of Faith movements. It teaches that God created man in His own image and that, therefore, Adam and Eve were little gods. When they disobeyed God in the Garden of Eden, they lost their deity and gave the dominion God had given to them over the earth to Satan. As a consequence, God lost sovereignty over the earth. This teaching goes on to say that when a person gives their life to Jesus, they become a little god again. The essence of this teaching is that God cannot intervene in the world unless He is first given permission to do so by us little gods. As little gods, the power of our words can speak things into existence, including our healing and wealth. If you speak the word of faith, it will come to pass. The blasphemy of this teaching is that God is robbed of His sovereignty in the world and can only act if He is first invited to act by us little gods who are now sovereign. The final outcome of all this is that, over time, the little gods will take dominion of the world away from Satan, creating a one world order of peace, harmony and love that sets itself up for the return of Jesus. This all sounds good, but is it biblical? No, not at all.

Such an approach places control of my healing firmly in the sovereignty of my own ability and not God's. My trust in God's sovereignty is reckoned to be a misapplication on my part, and therefore ineffectual. This approach robs me of my rest and peace in the sovereignty of God, leaving me to my own devices as I seek to try harder and harder in order to apply the right method through which I can *receive* my healing. However, since I believe that God is sovereign, I trust that He is always in control and can heal me anytime He so chooses. Either it is God's will for me to be healed or it is not. I have no mental strength to do battle with the will of God, thinking that I might somehow persuade Him, or bend His arm to heal me. The fact is, I can no more contribute to my healing than I can to my salvation.

There are too many examples of Christians for whom this self-effort mindset has not worked. Surely, this method is either foolproof and comes with a guarantee to *always* work, or it is not. I can think of leaders at the charismatic end of the church who have tried everything, believed everything, claimed everything, and yet they still died from their cancer. Are we to conclude that, in their case, nothing worked because Satan proved to be more powerful than Jesus? Are we to assume that they did not name and claim their healing enough or that they were perhaps exceptions to the rule?

While I most certainly believe in the power of God's word, I am not convinced that I can use it to tell God what to do. If I could, sovereignty is taken away from God and placed firmly under my control. I become sovereign and God has to submit Himself to my will and my efforts.

While God has not physically healed me, I take great comfort in the knowledge that Jesus has already healed me of the most hideous, destructive, deadly disease anyone can ever have: the spiritual disease of sin. Jesus did this for me at the cross:

> *'Surely He has borne our griefs and carried our sorrows;*
> *yet we esteemed him stricken, smitten by God, and afflicted.*
> *But He was pierced for our transgressions; He was crushed*

for our iniquities; upon him was the chastisement that brought us peace, and with his wounds we are healed' (Isa. 53: 4–5).

At the cross, Jesus triumphed over my sin and has brought me to a place of peace and rest in God. If Jesus has already healed me of the deadliest disease ever, He can most certainly heal me of cancer. My faith and trust in God are not dependent upon my physical healing or the removal of any other kind of calamity in my life. My greatest ever need in this life is not to be healed of cancer, but to be healed of the spiritual disease of sin and to be made right with God. My cancer reminds me that I live in a fallen world and a fallen body. It also reminds me of what God has rescued me from and that, one day, I will receive a completely new body made fit for life in God's eternal kingdom.

I trust, not that God is obliged to heal me, but that He will establish His purposes in His time. Faith trusts that God *always* knows what He is doing, and nothing can stop him from doing what He has decided to do or not to do. God has the power and authority to heal me or not to heal me. I am content to live with that.

Chapter 11

WHAT FAITH WILL NOT DO

Faith Does Not Give Me All the Answers

Beware of the person who claims to have all the answers to life. I place my faith firmly in Jesus, knowing that only He has all the answers. As God and Creator of all things, He knows everything and sees all things. He knows the end from the beginning. That is why I put my complete trust in Him and no one else, including myself. As much as I would like to have all the answers, I know that I do not. I do not *need* to know all the answers, but I do need to know Jesus as the one who knows it all and entrust myself to Him. Science does not have all the answers, but God does. God created science, and the scientists are simply trying to work out how God has designed everything and made it work.

Faith Will Not Give Me an Easy Ride

As we walk our journey of faith, there will be times when the road we travel is smooth, level and straight. At other times, the road may consist of steep ravines, excessive climbs and awkward twists and bends. There may be hazardous times when we suddenly hit a roadblock or a deep crater. Jesus never promised us a smooth, easy journey, and there will be times when the road we travel seems to become impassable and there is no way through. At such times, our journey of faith has the potential to become a journey of fear and panic. When we hit these insurmountable obstructions, we might find ourselves questioning whether this journey of faith is really worth it. If God wants us to get to the end of the journey, why does He allow the road to become seemingly impassable? We begin to ask God lots of questions and may very well discover that faith does not supply us with all the answers that we want.

Part of the reason I find myself writing this book is to ask what happens when our faith and trust in God does not match our hopes and expectations of God's leading, guiding, providing and protection. Since the Bible tells me that I am His child whom He loves and cares for, surely, He would treat me the same way as I treat my own children, whom I also love so very much? Surely, since I am God's child, He should do everything He can to make sure I have a safe, straightforward journey? What then, when God's love for me looks and feels like anything but loving? What happens when the road I travel gets so messed up and painful that I become despairingly frustrated and disillusioned to the point where I question whether I am even on the right road? It is at times like this when we are inclined to reason that faith does not work. This is precisely what Satan desires and encourages. He is bent on destroying my faith in Jesus and makes the most of any opportunities that come his way. The Apostle Peter writes in 1 Peter 5:6–9:

'Humble yourselves, therefore, under the mighty hand of God so that at the proper time he may exalt you, casting all your anxieties on him, because he cares for you. Be sober-minded; be watchful. Your adversary the devil prowls around like a roaring lion, seeking someone to devour. Resist him, firm in your faith, knowing that the same kinds of suffering are being experienced by your brotherhood throughout the world.'

Faith Will Not Prevent Me from Dying

Spiritual rebirth does not protect me from physical death, neither does it protect me from physical suffering. Faith does not nullify the fact that I live in a fallen, broken world. So many Christians throughout history have suffered terribly and continue to suffer persecution throughout the world because of their faith. In many cases, their faith has led to their painful, bloody execution. What is more, God has not rescued them! In the comfortable Westernized church, persecution is alien to our concept of a loving God and expectations of what it means to follow Christ. The truth is, if the death of a Christian does not arise from persecution, it will most certainly occur from natural causes.

You may be full to overflowing with faith, but that faith can never set aside the day of your bodily death. Even if we are blessed to live life in perfect health, all of us will eventually succumb to the ageing process. Even those TV evangelists, who preach health and wealth, cannot look in the mirror and name and claim back their youth! When was the last time you heard of a Christian asking God to heal them of the ageing process?

The truth is, Christians *must* shed this earthly body to make way for the new. In this respect, there is nothing strange about death. In the beginning, God did not create us to grow old and die, but due to the fall and curse in the Garden of Eden, death is now a natural occurrence and comes to us all. Should I feel cheated that I might not live to a ripe old age? No, I am so thankful to God for the 56 years of life He has given me so far. Many people live such short lives and die in their infancy, or as teenagers or young adults. I look at the day of my physical birth and thank God for that event. I did not ask or plan to be brought into this world, it had nothing to do with me whatsoever! The bottom line is this: I am so grateful that God formed me in my mother's womb and gave me life because my natural birth paved the way for my spiritual birth. In this sense, it doesn't really matter how long my earthly life might be; my physical birth made it possible for my spiritual birth to take place.

All of us are destined for death; how ever that may come. The longer we live, the older we become, and we begin to see the reality of our bodies wearing out and beginning to fail; no longer able to do what we did in our younger years because our ageing bodies will no longer cooperate! We can be certain that God will not heal us of growing old. It is said that with medical intervention, more people today are living into their nineties. Nevertheless, those of us who make it into those elderly years will eventually succumb to death by old age; the same fate overcomes everyone.

Many Christians pray for physical healing because sickness and disease do not represent God's blessing. This is most certainly true, and growing old is not a part of God's perfect kingdom. I am certain that given the choice, all of us would like to avoid the deterioration that accompanies old age, preferring to die by slipping away quickly and peacefully in our sleep before things get too uncomfortable. Normally speaking, we do not get to choose when, where or how we will die. We are forced to live with death's unpredictability since it can take a hold of us at any moment, young or old. All of us, without exception, live in the absolute certainty that while we are alive, we will continue to grow old. You can try as hard as you can to delay that process through eating well, keeping fit and avoiding everything that is harmful to your body, but you can never stop the onset of the ageing process. We live in the hope that we will spend our senior years living in peaceful tranquillity, catching up on things we have always wanted to do but never had the time, money or opportunity to do. None of us know how far we will get into the old age season, and so we approach it with uncertainty. We co-exist with a fear that wonders whether old age will treat us kindly, living in the hope that the day of our death will come before we ever lose our independence and dignity.

Faith cannot prevent anyone from dying, whether by some tragic accident, serious illness or old age. What faith in Jesus does do is conquer death because, on our behalf, Jesus conquered death through His own bodily resurrection. It is well worth reminding ourselves about the promise Jesus made in relation to the death of Lazarus:

> '*Martha said to Jesus; "Lord, if you had been here, my brother would not have died. But even now I know that whatever you ask from God, God will give you." Jesus said to her, "Your brother will rise again." Martha said to him, "I know that he will rise again in the resurrection on the last day." Jesus said to her, "I am the resurrection and the life. Whoever believes in me, though he die, yet shall he live, and everyone who lives and believes in me shall never die"'* (John 11:21–26).

Faith Always Works

The Death of a Believer

§

Part Two

FAITH EXPRESSED, SHAPED AND TESTED

Chapter 12

WHAT DOES FAITH SIGN ME UP FOR?

When we sign up to faith, how many of us actually know what we are signing up to? How many of us would still sign up if we knew that God was going to severely test and stretch our faith to the point of breaking us? How many of us would still sign up if we knew it was going to cost us everything we had, even our lives?

Christians who suffer serious life-changing sickness might ask why God leaves so many other Christians alone. Why pick on me and not others? It seems to me that the heavy hand of God has appointed some of His servants to suffer severe testing in order to train and teach them. Am I saying that God allows a person to suffer for their own good? Yes! Through suffering, God chooses to break some of His children for the purpose of bringing them to the end of themselves. He will use circumstances, sickness, poverty and other tragedies, doing whatever it takes to get His child to lay down their lives. Through suffering, they learn that survival depends upon submitting themselves wholly to the sovereignty of God and the need to depend entirely upon Him. Through suffering, God trains a person to be heavenly minded rather than earthly minded. The things of this world no longer hold any appeal, and they long for the presence of God more than anything that this world has to offer. They are the ones whom God almost takes out of the world yet keeps them in for the sake of His purposes and witness. Their witness is not about them, but about the one in whom they put their faith, trust and hope. When God allows or even ordains a Christian to suffer, they might begin to see things differently than they did before. In the case of a church leader, suffering might develop a mindset that is not afraid to challenge the church and call her to repentance for her slothful, unfaithful ways. These are leaders who no longer care about their own reputation or what makes them sound and look good. They are tired and weary of such things, recognizing how shallow they are. They are not people-pleasers who seek the approval of others by trying to win people over with entertainment or cleverness. God has knocked all of those worldly appeals and methods out of them so that they seek only to be faithful to what they know God has called them to be, and to do what only God can do.

Faith Signs Up for Persecution

The Apostle Paul writes:

> *'Anyone who desires to live a godly life in Christ Jesus will be persecuted'* (2 Tim. 2:12).

Paul strengthened and encouraged the churches in Lystra, Iconium and Antioch to:

> *'...continue in the faith, and saying that through many tribulations we must enter the kingdom of God'* (Acts 14:22).

Paul tells us (and he should know) that if a person commits to follow Christ, they must *expect* to suffer persecution. Following Christ will not render any one of us immune from suffering ridicule or oppression. Some Christians might say that they can avoid such suffering by getting on with the world so as not to offend it, but this is not what the Bible teaches. At some point in time, true faith will clash with the belief systems and morality of the world, since we are dealing with two different kingdoms that oppose each other and can never be united. While Christians still live in the world, they are no longer of it. The time will inevitably come when a Christian will be called to stand up and be counted, simply because there is a division that separates a person of true faith and a person who has no faith. Such division can never be united and can lead to strife,

anger, hatred, accusation, intolerance and disharmony, not at all
meaning by the one who has faith, but the one who does not. Such
a schism is bound to occur where there exists this partition,
including in one's own family. Jesus said:

> *'Brother will deliver brother over to death, and the father*
> *his child, and children will rise against parents and have*
> *them put to death and you will be hated by all for my name's*
> *sake. But the one who endures to the end will be saved'*
> (Matt. 10:21–22).

I do not think there are many Christians in the contemporary
Western church who are willing to take the above verses seriously,
because their idea of Christianity is all about being happy in this
life and getting on with the world and being liked. Is this how
Jesus lived?

The time is already at hand, where those who *'seek first the
kingdom of God and his righteousness'* will be judged to be
extremely offensive, accused of hate speech, intolerance and of
being unlawful. I am especially thinking of those aspects of life
that relate to all areas to do with sexuality, marriage and the family
construct that God has ordained to shape the backbone of a healthy
society. A time is coming when the church will be enforced not
only to accept secular ideologies but to endorse and promote them.
While there are tough times ahead for the true church, God will
ultimately provide a heavenly blessing to those who faithfully
endure suffering of whatever nature, with an eternal reward that
will far outweigh their momentary troubles. (2 Cor. 4:17)

Faith does not sign me up for a happy life in this world. Instead, it
signs me up for the joy of my salvation in Christ. Faith does not
sign me up to belong to a church establishment or organization
per se; it signs me up to Christ because I belong to Him and not to
this world. Every true Christian is happy to be set apart from this
world because they no longer fit into this world but stand out as
someone who is prepared to lose their reputation and life as they
follow Christ.

Chapter 13

FAITH AND THE LOCAL CHURCH

First and foremost, faith signs me up to Christ and the committing of myself to Him. By association, the secondary effect of my commitment to Christ signs me up to the *global* church, which is united in Christ who is the Head of the church. The Bible teaches that the church is Christ's visible body on earth that is given human form and expression through each body member of the church. That body is brought to life by the indwelling Holy Spirit whom God has given to unite each individual, to help and empower the church to bear witness to Christ throughout the whole world.

The history of the church since the time of the Apostles has been a bloody one, not just from external persecution but also from internal confrontations. Since about AD 312, the church came under the increasing acceptance and influence of a declining Roman empire, which morphed into what we know to be the Roman Catholic church. In 1517, the Reformation came into being through various courageous and determined men who challenged the authority and practices of the Catholic church, together with her domineering claim of authority through which she insisted that salvation can only come through her. The Reformers were prepared to be executed by Rome for their opposition, through which they set out to make the Bible available to the ordinary lay person, rather than restricted to the Rome-appointed Bishops and Priests who insisted it remained in its Latin form and therefore kept hidden from the general public. The reformation led to Protestantism, which in turn has given birth to all the different worldwide denominational churches that we have today.

While faith signs me up to the global church, it especially signs me up to the *local* church. The local church is a community of faith where that faith is given corporate expression in a localized setting. Here, the gospel is preached, the Bible taught, and praise and prayer offered up to God. Each member of the local church has a part to play in the life of that local church. According to each member's spiritual and practical gifting, the members encourage each other to grow stronger in their faith and build each other up. In a very real sense, the local church is just like a family. As in any family, there is a bond of love and commitment that comes from the unity of being yoked together in Christ, regardless of ethnicity and gender.

Who is the Church For?

Over the last 40 years or so, I have watched the growing range of independent Christian movements which have sprung up in protest at the formality that is found in the traditional, institutional, established church. Such formality is seen to be lifeless, emotionless, boring, pointless, irrelevant, ineffective, ageing, in decline and going nowhere. These movements have taken a fresh approach that creates a movement that has a wider appeal, making it a lot easier for anyone to belong to. Such movements include the seeker-friendly and progressive type churches, which have become extremely successful by appealing to the ever-changing culture of today that is looking for something alternative. Their target audience is especially the younger generations who have energy, enthusiasm and youth on their side. They often grow into mega-churches that have created their own brand of celebrity leaders. Their influence is huge, growing a worldwide network of smaller para-church movements that operate under their umbrella.

In all of this, I believe that the big question that needs to be asked is: Who is the church for? Obviously, the church is made up entirely of saved sinners, but what about the focal point of the church, which is her weekly gathering together on a Sunday? I imagine that most of the newer movements that have arisen in recent years would say that, for the sake of evangelism, these gatherings should primarily be aimed at the un-churched, an event which Christians are not embarrassed to invite their non-Christian friends to without them feeling out of place or uncomfortable. In a very real sense, the church invites the world into the church. Some might say that this should be what church is all about, removing barriers and promoting a safe place in which the world feels accepted and not threatened in any way. Yet there is a casualty in all of this, namely that the absolute truth of God's written word cannot be preached, and the church's message and worship become dumbed down, leading to compromise.

The Greek word for 'church' is *ecclesia,* which is defined as 'an assembly' or 'called out ones', meaning the assembling together of those who have been called out of the world and into God's kingdom. To my mind, Sunday church is for the church and aimed at the church. It is aimed primarily at those who already have faith and are learning how to follow Christ, who want to gather together as the body of Christ to worship God, feed on the truth of God's word, hear the gospel preached, pray together, and are then sent out into the week ahead, to bear witness to the gospel message of salvation in Christ within the context of the world in which they live. In this Sunday assembly, there is a deliberate gathering for the mutual edification and the building up of one another in the faith. Of course, there is nothing to stop non-Christians from attending church, and the doors of the church must always be wide open and welcoming to those who have no faith. This is what makes the preaching of the gospel message of salvation each Sunday so essential, for the sake of building up those who have faith while convicting those who have no faith.

Chapter 14

ONE CHURCH OR MANY?

There is a whole host of different types of churches out there from which to choose. It all depends upon which brand ticks your box, for example:

The Mega-Church

This is the church where numbers are everything. The perception is that bigger is better, giving the appearance of being successful, going somewhere and doing something. Bigger churches can do so many things since they have more resources at their disposal. One of the major draws to these big churches is their ability to put on big worship and high-tech visuals, creating a buzz and a charged-up, experiential atmosphere that helps to pull in the crowds.

Many of the mega-churches are driven by celebrity pastors who have the charisma to draw in the crowds. More often than not, these churches are likely to have a Charismatic or Pentecostal flavour to them, promoting a prosperity gospel that teaches it is always God's will for a person to be healthy, wealthy and successful. The Charismatic movement is a big fish that is heavily influenced by the Word of Faith and so-called New Apostolic Reformation movements. They are likely to hold to a 'Kingdom Now' theology that believes the church will establish God's kingdom on earth in preparation for the return of Christ. For this doctrine to be credible, it necessitates an eschatology which believes that we are already in the millennial period and that Christ is already reigning on earth through His church. The attractiveness of such teaching is that as children of King Jesus, we have all of the privileges and benefits of our royalty right now; we simply need to recognize who we are in Christ and our royal status. Needless to say, such a message keeps the mega-church growing.

I do not blame the crowds for wanting it all now; who wouldn't? However, I believe that the Scriptures teach that this will not materialize until Christ the King returns to set up and establish His kingdom on earth. In Revelation 21:3–5, we see what His eternal kingdom will look like:

> *'And I heard a loud voice from the throne saying, "Behold, the dwelling place of God is with man. He will dwell with them, and they will be his people, and God himself will be with them as their God. He will wipe away every tear from their eyes, and death shall be no more, neither shall there be mourning, nor crying, nor pain anymore, for the former things have passed away." And he who was seated on the throne said, "Behold, I am making all things new."'*

The Worship Experience

A fundamental feature in the majority of mega-churches is what's known as the worship experience. An atmosphere is created that resemble the vibes of a secular rock concert, which strike a chord with the worshipper's feelings and emotions. However, our feelings and emotions are untrustworthy, unreliable, and easily manipulated. Create the right atmosphere, and the impression is given that something spiritual is taking place, yet nothing could be further from the truth. A person's faith, based on feelings and emotions, is easily attracted by the wrong motives and open to physiological and even hypnotic abuse. Is God impressed with us when we jump up and down, wave our arms in the air, shake, and look like we are out of control? I do not think so. God looks at the heart to see if we are worshipping Him in spirit and in truth. They are the worshippers that the Father seeks (John 4:23). The writer of Hebrews wrote:

> *'Let us offer to God acceptable worship, with reverence and awe'* (Heb. 12:28).

The Apostle Paul teaches us to:

'Present your bodies as a living sacrifice, holy and acceptable to God, which is your spiritual worship' (Rom. 12:1).

The defence is made that the worship experience is relevant to today's contemporary world and a necessary evangelistic tool. Even so, I can't but help think that if the music and lights were taken away and replaced by an honest, biblical gospel message, how many of those worshippers would soon disappear? I am particularly disturbed by the worship some churches open themselves up to. These churches are more concerned with experiences rather than with biblical doctrine. Their focus is primarily on the Holy Spirit rather than on Jesus Christ, a focus that determines their approach to an evangelism that necessitates a Holy Spirit encounter, signs and wonders, getting drunk and slain in the Spirit, soaking up the Spirit's anointing and impartations of the Spirit's power from one person to the next. All of these things are manipulations which go above and beyond what the Scriptures teach us.

The Successful Church

What qualifies any given church to be reckoned a success? Is it the number of people who attend, the number of water baptisms held, the sophistication of the technical equipment used, the size of the stage or the credibility of the worship band and the influence of the celebrity pastor?

Many church leaders strive to appear successful since this is seen as a sign of God's approval and presence. The main thrust of its teachings focuses on success, happiness and a fulfilment that can be found in the material things that this world has to offer. The degree of faith one has is reflected by the wealth, health, success and spiritual anointing one has. Understandably, this is a very attractive message that appeals to many people.

The Easy-Going, Attractive Church

Traditional, orthodox Christianity is not an eye-catching, sexy product, so the contemporary church of today has tried to change all of that. Consequently, she has resorted to all kinds of marketing gimmicks, latest fads and trends in a bid to sell herself and make herself attractive. Image is everything, and the attractive church dresses herself up so that she looks good, feels good and sounds good. This is a church that focuses on the felt needs of the individual and how to be a better, happier you. It is non-confrontational, easy on the ears and promotes a feel-good gospel that is formulated to build up self-esteem.

The Business-Run Church

As soon as a church finds her identity in a building, she runs the risk of being run like a business. Committees are set up, visions cast, methods formulated, programmes developed, and agendas fixed. The bigger the church, the greater need there is for more structure and organization. Everything is programmed to run smoothly in order to keep ahead, busy, attractive, marketable and on target.

The Liberal Church

The culture of today promotes an all-inclusive and equality-driven society. This can be both a good thing and a bad thing. The liberal church works hard to replicate this and promote an ecumenical church that embraces the beliefs of other faiths as being equal and valid. Since there is already so much negativity, doom and gloom in the world, the message proclaimed is one that celebrates the goodness to be found in humanity. Its message is always positive and upbeat. The thrust of the liberal's message is that God's love is unconditional and that He loves you just the way you are. Her gospel is a social-driven, social justice gospel that promotes a united, peaceful, prosperous, more hope-filled society and a new world order. The goal is a big one that works towards eradicating hunger, poverty, social injustice, inequality, hatred and intolerance.

The Worldly Church

All of the above movements and organizations share many of the same characteristics and aspirations. There is a large crossover of the same basic message which they all promote and endorse. In particular, they attract the younger generations, who are keen to be a part of a popular movement that seeks to change the world into a better place to live. Unfortunately, what most of the churches above all have in common is that they have, one way or another, become a worldly church. Within them, there is much which is good and right, but there is a lot that is harmful, misleading, distracting and false.

The church today in the West is being put to the test, but it is not through persecution; rather, it is through the pressure to adapt to a fast-changing progressive culture that is doing away with the absolutes of the past and the structure of how God created everything to work in harmony. As the church attempts to fit in and work with the culture, she finds herself on a relentless path that lays aside the authority of the Bible together with its truths, teachings and doctrines. The Apostle Paul wrote:

> '*All Scripture is God-breathed and is useful for instruction, for conviction, for correction, and for training in righteousness, so that the man of God may be complete, fully equipped for every good work*' (2 Tim. 3:16–17).

When the teaching of the Bible is no longer considered to be the authoritative word of God, a worldly church is produced. Preaching from the Bible gives way to the attractive opinions of trendy motivational speakers, who consider themselves to be supremely spiritual, culturally relevant and progressive. Worship is no longer seen to be a way of life but is made manifest in the liveliness and emotionalism of the Sunday gatherings. The

Sunday service is replaced by the Sunday experience, whose top priority is designed to make a person feel good about themselves so that they keep coming back for more. I view these things as nothing more than DIY Christianity, which makes the mistake of thinking that God is impressed by the same things that impress the world. It is not so much the world invading the church, but the church inviting the world into the church for the sake of popularity.

I would most certainly agree that promoting equality and the eradication of hunger, poverty, injustice, hatred and intolerance are excellent goals and worthy of the church's witness in the world, but no amount of good social activity and best intentions dressed up in Christian clothes can eradicate the root problem to all of these things. Good works are good but can never be a substitute for the proclamation of the true gospel that tells a person the truth about God and themselves. For example, the social gospel will not tell a person that their sin not only condemns them and separates them from God but places them under His judgment. The social gospel will not tell a person that their most urgent, desperate need in this life is to repent of their sin and get right with God through faith in Jesus and why. As I see it, the worldly church dares not preach an honest gospel for fear of offending people and scaring them away. Herein lies the biggest danger of all. If the true honest gospel is not preached, a half gospel is preached that produces a faith that is self-centred and falls right into the hands of the 'me-ism' agenda which is so prevalent in today's culture. Here's the thing; me-ism is what most people need to be saved from. At stake here is not just what the worldly church teaches but what it does not teach. The worldly church creates a worldly faith that is built upon nothing more than the shifting sands of insecurity and instability of an ever-changing culture. Because of her seeker-friendly, all-inclusive approach, her leaders have to adapt to a new selective gospel that suits the message they want to send out to today's modern mind.

The Selective Church

The lack of biblical teaching in the church means that the worldly church is rendered powerless because it does not deal with the root cause of humanities problem, which is spiritual. It does away with the biblical message of the cross and consequently loses its heart, soul and purpose. In order to attract new converts, the popular, all-inclusive church is forced to endorse an easy evangelism that makes it as easy as possible for someone to become a Christian and enter the Kingdom. Easy evangelism promotes a Christianity that is all about me and my self-esteem. As a result, it has to do away with the barbarism of hell, sin and God's judgment since these things are considered to be too negative, offensive and out of date. Consequently, the Bible is watered down, ignoring its teachings such as sin, hell and God's judgment while going straight to the good news. That good news is that Jesus loves you, wants you to be happy and wants you to go to heaven when you die because you are so special, and you are worth it! Whatever elements of truth are included in this easy message, it is not the *whole* truth. It is a half-truth aimed directly towards the emotions and feelings, rather than to challenge and stir the mind.

I cannot reconcile any of this to the proclamation of the good news as presented in the Bible. The biblical way sets out to reveal the bad news first before proclaiming the good news (much as I have done in this book). Without an understanding of the reality and effects of sin, the Holy Spirit cannot bring about the conviction of a person's sin and its most hideous consequences. Only when a person understands the bad news with their mind does the offer of good news provide relief or make any sense. The bad news followed by the good news is what brings about a genuine repentance that understands what sin is and why it needs to be repented of. Understanding the bad news fuels the desire and sense of urgency to get right with God and trust in Jesus to save a person from their sin.

The result of easy evangelism and selective Bible-teaching robs people of having any effective concept of the seriousness of what sin is and what it leads to. Due to biblical illiteracy, many do not really know what following Jesus really means or see the need to take God seriously. Many do not have a biblical understanding of the holiness of God or the need to be Holy as God is Holy (Heb. 12:14). Many do not understand how necessary repentance is, and that repentance is not just a matter of saying sorry for all the bad things but a turning away from a life of sin which offends God. Needless to say, much of the contemporary church is filled with people who are willing to associate or belong to a church but unknowingly never become what Christ intended His followers to be. The sparsity of authoritative, authentic Bible-teaching has led to a church that has grown accustomed to an easy, smooth ride. Theology, which is the study of the nature and character of God, is not taken seriously and neglected, leading to a warped view and understanding of the true nature of God. The most people can tolerate is what I would call Sunday school theology, a theology that causes no offence and makes no demands.

Above Scripture

Thus, the contemporary, worldly church does not place herself under the authority of the truth of God's word as revealed in Scripture. While the Bible is not completely abandoned, a lot of its content is either distorted or ignored, deemed to be divisive and lacking credibility. To get over this, the Bible is re-interpreted and given a new flavour that is palatable for today's sophisticated, intellectual, scientific, forward-thinking and open-minded culture. What is offered is a reconstructed, up-to-date, attractive message that deconstructs the validity of the original gospel message that was proclaimed by the early church and recorded for us by the Apostles in Scripture. A progressive gospel is produced that is not based on the Bible but on what feels is acceptable to modern-day sensitivities. The Apostle James issues a warning to those who desire to have a prominent voice within the church:

'Not many of you should become teachers, my brothers, for you know that we who teach will be judged with greater strictness' (James 3:1).

98

The quest to relegate the Bible in order to elevate today's cultural opinions reveals a dissatisfaction and a vote of no confidence in what the Bible has to say. The implications of this relegation result in a church that is really no different from the world that she is trying to reach. In one sense, the church is offering what the world already has, but with Jesus tagged on. She has thrown away her unique witness and testimony that sets her apart as being the counter-cultural witness that God has called her out from the world to be. Yet the message of the Bible is that the Bible-based church has something incredibly good to offer the world, something that the world does not already have and can never attain through her own wisdom or philosophies. No one has been commissioned by Jesus to do their own thing, but to proclaim the gospel message of salvation as revealed in Scripture.

As I see it, the validity of the Bible will continue to come under increasing attack, not only by society and culture but especially from within the ranks of the compromised, progressive church. In order to protect her credibility, and for fear of being seen to commit intellectual suicide, there is an agenda from within the church to change the gospel that was handed down to her by the Apostles. When I look at the mindset of the world, I am in no way surprised or confused, since I know where that mindset is coming from and why. On the other hand, when I look at the mindset of much of today's church, I am left confused, puzzled and grieved. The solid doctrines of the Bible that informs, teaches, rebukes, reforms and transforms are being swept away to make way for the pragmatic approach of whatever feels right and appears to work.

What Happened to Sin, Hell and Judgment?

The most damaging and dangerous aspect to the deconstruction and reconstruction of the Bible by contemporary evangelicalism is that the fundamental truths of how to be saved from sin are being neglected. Teaching about sacrifice, cost, humility, repentance, judgment, suffering and hell are considered alien concepts to the sophisticated minds of today. The biblical concept of sin and the cross is an embarrassment, yet this is the unique message that the church has to offer and what the world needs to hear. The Apostle Paul told the newly formed church in Corinth to preach Christ crucified and then went on to say:

> '...but we preach Christ crucified, a stumbling block to Jews and folly to the Gentiles, but to those who are called, both Jews and Greeks, Christ the power of God and the wisdom of God' (1 Cor. 1:23–24).

Nonetheless, the worldly church in her wisdom thinks differently. She has lost confidence in the power of God's word for salvation and the power of the Holy Spirit to bring about conviction of sin and repentance. Instead, the worldly church places confidence in her own wisdom and methodology to win people over and keep them there. Her message offers a quick-fix faith and an easy short cut into 'the kingdom'. However, no one will ever get into the kingdom of God by the back door of an attractive quick fix. No one can drift into the kingdom or enter in by simply reciting the sinner's prayer. Jesus said:

> 'From the days of John the Baptist until now the kingdom of heaven has suffered violence and the violent take it by force' (Matt.11:12).

In the above verse, the violent are those who are eager and zealous to grasp hold of the kingdom, to take possession of it and hold onto it. In Matthew 13:44–46, Jesus told two parables:

> 'The kingdom of heaven is like treasure hidden in a field, which a man found and covered up. Then in his joy he goes and sells all that he has and buys that field. Again, the kingdom of heaven is like a merchant in search of fine pearls, who, on finding one pearl of great value, went and sold all that he had and bought it'

The truth is, we are all born into the wide way that leads to a life outside of the kingdom. The kingdom can only be entered through a deliberate, intentional effort to enter through the narrow door that leads to life (Luke 13:24 & Matt. 7:13–14). This door is the front door of the cross of Jesus, who is the King of the kingdom and from where real faith always begins and from where it continues to live, grow and thrive. It is sad to say that a quick fix has led many people into believing that they are in the kingdom when they are not. They go to church, sing the songs and pray the prayers but are not among the few who enter. In contrast to the few, Jesus taught about the many:

> *'On that day many will say to me, 'Lord, Lord, did we not prophesy in your name, and cast out demons in your name, and do many mighty works in your name?' And then will I declare to them, 'I never knew you; depart from me, you workers of lawlessness'* (Matt. 7:22–23).

Perhaps the most powerful delusion promoted by a growing number of secularized, liberal churches is that they focus entirely on God's love. That last sentence might sound a bit of an odd thing for me to pick up on; after all, isn't God's love what salvation is all about? Yes, it most certainly is, and the immensity, power and extravagance of God's love are way beyond our ability to fully comprehend. That being said, God's love cannot be separated from God's other attributes that include His justice and wrath. The Bible and Jesus do not make this separation, and nor should we. The Bible teaches us that God is very angry and offended by our sin. It is precisely because God is complete in His perfection, goodness and holiness, that He cannot overlook sin. A growing number of well-known evangelical leaders are giving credence to the idea of universalism and that the power of God's love is so strong and unconditional that, in the end, He will save everyone from hell and for heaven. All you need to do is to realize and understand how much God loves and accepts you, so that you can be empowered to love yourself and those around you. Such love, they say, would create a society and a world that can live in peace, harmony, prosperity and abundance. No more wars, food shortages, hatred and division; a kind of utopia! In my opinion, any global peace plan widely misses the mark and seeks to do what only God can do. We cannot work with God on our terms but only on His terms.

As I have said before, what is so misleading about this approach is not so much about what it teaches but what it does *not* teach. This method is counter-productive, since it actually leads more people away from heaven and into hell. If God's love means that He cannot resist but save everyone, then what is the point in preaching the biblical gospel message of salvation? It becomes a meaningless exercise. There is no need for a response to the gospel message because there is no gospel message that needs to be responded to; it is made redundant! Jesus, they say, went to the cross simply to demonstrate the greatest expression of God's love, thus setting for us the supreme example of what it means to love one another. I believe that such an approach is a hideous and mocking offence to what Jesus accomplished at the cross, creating a deceptive warped view of 'Jesus loves you'. I would even go as far as to say that I believe it is helping to pave the way for the end-time great apostasy that will manifest the abandonment, rebellion and a great falling away from the *truth* of God's word. What is so remarkable is that this apostasy takes place from *within* the church and is one of the key signs that the end time is very near. (2 Thess. 2:1–12)

No Distinction

I dare to say that by attempting to gain the approval of the world, the worldly church has lost the approval of God. As I read the New Testament, my understanding is that while the church is in the world, she is to function as a light in a dark place because she is no longer of the world. Yet today's worldly church is very much in coalition with the world. Instead of the church being counter-cultural, she is pro-cultural and has redefined the biblical concept and meaning of what is right and what is wrong. As a result, there is very little distinction between the worldly church that holds to a secular worldview and a secular society that does not know or love God. This lack of distinction has come about because the worldly church twists what the Bible teaches to make it say what they want it to say. Yet the Bible presents a gospel and way of life that *is* distinctive, calling for the death to self and the surrender of all to Christ. This is the narrow way that leads to life, whereas much of the contemporary church has made that way much wider so that she appeals to many more people who can travel on the wide way. Jesus once said:

> *'Enter by the narrow gate. For the gate is wide and the way is easy that leads to destruction, and those who enter by it are many. For the gate is narrow and the way is hard that leads to life, and those who find it are few'* (Matt. 7:13–14).

Eastern Mysticism

In addition to all of the above elements that make up much of today's church, there is a growing interest within the church that embraces certain forms of eastern mysticism. These come in the shape of practising such things as; meditation, visualization, Christ consciousness, prayer centering, emptying the mind, getting in touch with your higher self, out of body and transcendent experiences and much more. All of these things fool people into thinking they are encountering some kind of spiritual experience that is from God, whereas what they are actually opening themselves up to are demonic influences. One such influence is the Kundalini spirit that awakens the body to other-worldly experiences such as spiritual transportations and divine visions. This is precisely why churches should not embrace the practice of yoga since it is the doorway that leads into eastern mysticism.

Church Under Threat

Throughout the whole of church history, God has been calling the *true* church out of the world so that she can stand out and be better identified. In today's secularized West, society, culture and governments are demonizing and even criminalizing orthodox Christianity, seeing it as something that is harmful to the progress of global unity and the 'Great Reset' that paves the way for a progressive new world order. This presents a significant threat to the true church, who desperately need church leaders who are prepared to stand out and speak the true gospel message, proving themselves to be true servants and shepherds over Christ's flock. The church of today must cry out for courageous, counter-cultural leaders who will provide the spiritual discernment so urgently needed in these days in which spiritual deception has been allowed to thrive.

> *'For the time is coming when people will not endure sound teaching, but having itching ears they will accumulate for themselves teachers to suit their own passions, and will turn away from listening to the truth and wander off into myths'* (2 Tim. 4:3–4).

There are only two kingdoms that have eternal significance: the kingdom of God and the kingdom of Satan, the kingdom of light and the kingdom of darkness. This fallen world falls into the category of Satan's kingdom, offering so much that is designed to make us feel good about ourselves. However, Jesus said that His kingdom is not of this world. He made it very clear that His kingdom and this world are directly opposed to each other. We cannot serve the kingdom of God and the kingdom of this world. We cannot serve both, love both or live in both. Christ calls us *out* of the world, to be set apart *from* the world, and for Him. This is a fundamental requisite that bears testimony to our Christian witness. I recently came across my dad's old Bible and discovered a scrap of paper stuck onto the first page. It was something said by William Booth:

> *I consider the chief dangers that confronts the coming century will be;*
> *Religion without the Holy Ghost,*

Christianity without Christ,
Forgiveness without repentance,
Salvation without regeneration,
Politics without God,
Heaven without hell.

An increasing number of churches today promote a spirituality which has more to do with carnality, mysticism and New Age practices. Since these things are dressed up in Christian clothes and Christian jargon, more and more people are being deceived by its seduction, unable to differentiate between the Holy Spirit and false spirits. The backbone of this new progressive Christianity is the belief that Christianity has been evolving ever since the Day of Pentecost and that the New Testament can now be unhinged from the Old Testament. They say that such progression must be welcomed and understood to be God's new revelation for us in the world of today.

Chapter 15

THE AUTHENTIC CHURCH

Unless the LORD builds the house, those who build it labour in vain (Psalm 127:1).

Many people talk of 'going to church', but the church is not a building. The buildings used are static, dead and do not go to heaven! The true church is alive and lives in every area of society, consisting of those people who have placed their faith and trust in Jesus. These are disciples of Jesus Christ who live out their faith in their everyday lives, wherever God has placed them. Sadly, there are many Christians who do not see the need to belong to their local church. While it is most certainly true that going to church does not make anyone a Christian, belonging to a local church is an outward sign that demonstrates someone to be a Christian. Seeing no need to commit to a local church bears witness to a serious contradiction, since commitment to Christ and the local church go hand in hand. How can anyone be committed to one and not the other?

As Christians, we should examine why we belong to any particular church. Did we join for the right reasons? Is it because of the quality of the coffee and the trendy looking lounge, the contemporary ambience and the buzz created by the crowd around us? Did we decide on a church based only on what we can get out of it?

In light of what I have said about the modern-day church in the West, you might wonder why I am making such a big deal about what kind of church a Christian should belong to. I believe it to be very important since a church that is spiritually unhealthy produces and maintains unhealthy Christians. What is at stake is the matter of authenticity, where an authentic church produces authentic Christians who personify the authentic Christ in a sinful world.

The Faithful Church

There is always going to be a marked difference between the faithful and the unfaithful church, both of which cannot stand united. With this in mind, there is no such thing as the perfect church, since even the faithful church is made up of imperfect sinners, all of whom *have* been saved, *are* being saved and *will* be saved by God's grace.

So how does anyone choose which church to belong to? Is it just a matter of finding a church that suits our age, our children, taste, outlook, personality, circumstances, locality and the like? No doubt we take all of these factors into consideration, but they are not to be our number one consideration in selecting a church. Our priority needs to be given to the *faithful* church: the church that exists for the glory of Christ alone. It is the church that places herself under the *whole* counsel of God's written word, nothing more, nothing less. It is the church which proclaims the *honest* gospel message of salvation that bears testimony to the crucified and risen Lord Jesus Christ. The faithful church produces faithful disciples who are full of faith and are prepared to pick up their cross and follow in the footsteps of Jesus, no matter what the cost. The faithful church is the Spirit-filled church, who by His influence, leading and presence makes plain the focus of worship and preaching that is centred upon Jesus.

The Relevant Church

The authentic, faithful church is none other than the relevant church, so what does a relevant church look like? It is a church that is full of faithful obedience to Christ and is filled and empowered by the Holy Spirit, evidenced especially in the arena of witness and Holy living. The relevant church always points to Jesus Christ.

The relevancy of a local church does not depend upon her size. A large church that continues to grow in number does not necessarily indicate that the church is relevant in the right way, or who is producing the spiritual fruit God is looking for. It is possible that a large, thriving and lively church is a compromised church, no longer proclaiming the challenging, authentic gospel message handed down by the Apostles and which drives a lot of people away. It is possible that a church is large in number because she proclaims an easy-going, social-driven gospel that sets out to please everyone and makes no demands. On the other hand, I would go as far as to say that perhaps a faithful church is likely to be a small church because it is full of uncompromised followers of Jesus, who are prepared to be seen as unpopular because of their authentic faith.

A Christian who belongs to a church for the right reasons is the one who wants to play their part rather than be entertained. They want to encourage and build up others in their faith as well as their own and to be supportive of the presence of the church within their local community. It is to belong and be a part of the faithful and relevant church, which is the church that Jesus speaks of:

'And I tell you, you are Peter, and on this rock I will build my church, and the gates of hell shall not prevail against it' (Matt. 16:18).

Chapter 16

THE TESTING OF FAITH

The value or trustworthiness of anything is not known until it has been tried and tested. The testing of anything *proves* whether something is genuine or not, whether it is working properly and does what it is supposed to do. Faith is no different.

The Testing of Faith Shapes Faith

Once God gives to us the gift of faith to believe in Jesus, He begins to work with it. He shapes it, prunes it, refines it, grows it and tests it through everyday life. We may *learn* about faith in a Sunday sermon and through the study of God's word, but faith is developed, grown, shaped and proved, as it is *applied* out there in the real world. That is a real faith that lives in the real world, a world in which we struggle with all manner of temptations, trials and tough times that come our way. It is the world in which we have to make choices in how we spend our time and money and what we devote ourselves to. Everything that we do, say, think and desire reflects the faith we possess.

Does God Test all Faith, Weak or Strong?

At some point in time, God will see to it that our faith is tested. The truth is, the moment a person's faith is born, their faith will be tested as soon as they step out of their front door, surf the internet or spend time with their non-Christian friends. When faith has just been born, it is probably at its weakest and most vulnerable. Faith will need all the encouragement and support it can get. The moment we first become a Christian, God gives to us the Holy Spirit to help grow and establish our faith. We are not immediately given a super-faith that can endure anything and everything. Severe testing might destroy a newborn faith, causing it to fail and fall at the first hurdle. Perhaps God tends to shield such newly formed babies in the faith since their faith needs to be protected and nurtured for a while. Perhaps God waits until our faith has been strengthened before He allows our faith to be tested to any significant degree.

Testing not only matures faith but proves its authenticity. When the time of testing does come, our faith will be stretched, causing it to grow and become stronger, just like a muscle. As the Apostle Paul teaches: *'Be watchful, stand firm in the faith, act like men, be strong'* (1 Cor. 16:13). It is not God's will or expectation for any of us to settle for a weak faith. A faith that remains weak remains vulnerable. Our knowledge of theology and doctrine can be easily tested by sitting a paper examination, and yet the testing of faith is not a test that can be examined in such a way. Rather, faith is put to the test by the fiery trials that take place in the reality of real life. It can be very painful and has the potential to destroy us. God's motive is not to punish or destroy us but to refine, purify and prune us. If our faith is genuine, we can expect God to take us through the fire, not because He wants us to suffer, but to make us more fruitful so that we possess a faith that can serve Him better. It is not as though God does not know how genuine our faith is, for He knows all things. The testing serves to reveal to ourselves and others what kind of a faith we have.

Whenever my faith has been tested, I have become more aware of my spiritual shortcomings and weaknesses. I see how faithless I can be, and this shows up the sin I still have in my life. Romans 14:23 makes the point that whenever we doubt God, our doubting does not proceed from faith. It goes on to say that *'whatever does not proceed from faith is sin.'* So, if we doubt God in what we do, say or think, we sin against God. If I doubt God in any way, I sin against Him because I cannot sin against God as an act of faith. This is why, when my faith is put to the test, my lack of faith comes to light and the sin in me that produces that lack of faith is revealed by my doubt. Yet God uses the recognition of my

110

weaknesses and failings to get me to acknowledge my ongoing dependency upon the sufficiency of His eternal grace. His grace is far more powerful than my failings and so His grace never condemns me but always gives me hope and spiritual strength.

Faith is Put to the Test Every Day

My faith is put to the test every day in a world that does not share the faith that I have. I live in England, which used to be considered a Christian country, but not anymore. Since the 1960s, England has steadily thrown away whatever Christian heritage she once had for a more exciting, enticing, liberal secularism. In today's England there is a profound lack of faith. From the moment I get out of bed in the morning till the moment I return at night, my faith is tested by everything outside of me: by other people, circumstances and the temptations and difficulties of everyday life.

Storms Will Come

Jesus once told this parable:

'Everyone then who hears these words of mine and does them will be like a wise man who built his house on the rock. And the rain fell, and the floods came, and the winds blew and beat on that house, but it did not fall, because it had been founded on the rock. And everyone who hears these words of mine and does not do them will be like a foolish man who built his house on the sand. And the rain fell, and the floods came, and the winds blew and beat against that house, and it fell, and great was the fall of it' (Matt. 7:24–27).

This warning teaches me that Jesus knows that storms will come to us all, whether we place our faith in Him or not. We may all be hit by the same storm, but the outcome for the one who has a genuine faith in Jesus is very different from the one who has no faith, or a superficial faith. While a person's faith does not exempt them from the storm, their faith in Jesus does exempt them from spiritual collapse and destruction.

What Does the Testing of Faith Reveal?

The testing of our faith will reveal what kind of faith we really have. Whenever anyone is tested, it is the faith they possess at that moment in time which is being tested, not the faith they wished they had or once had in the past. Testing will always test the quality, depth, strength and authenticity of the faith we possess in the present.

A Negative Outcome

If the faith we possess is superficial and shallow, testing has the potential to produce a negative response. Instead of drawing us closer to God so that we take refuge in Him, we turn away from Him and take refuge in anything else that will provide us with the comfort and relief that we seek. This is a very slippery slope that can lead us into sitting in judgment over God, blaming Him for failing us and letting us down. We accuse Him of unfairness and foul play. Instead of making us happy, He has made us very unhappy and has proved Himself to be unreliable and not at all trustworthy. We sit in judgment over Him for not living up to our expectations, deeming Him to be undeserving of our approval and acceptance. We begin to ask those big questions that are designed to call God to account, such as, how can a God of love allow the innocent to suffer? We ask bigger questions that are designed to justify ourselves in our condemnation of God; How can a good God send anyone to hell for all eternity? We ask further questions that are designed to justify ourselves while criticizing God for being so irresponsible in the first place. For example, why did God allow His perfect creation to be so utterly ruined by a fallen angel whom He created in the first place: where is the sense or logic in that? Was God not powerful or loving enough to protect us and prevent any of this bad stuff from happening? Did He not think through the implications of the consequential suffering and misery that has been inflicted upon the whole of human history and creation? Why did God allow Satan such freedom?

Actually, all of those questions are legitimate questions that we need to face up to. If we ask them with a lack of awareness of how unlike God we are, we will judge Him according to our own standards and reasoning of how things ought to be. That is not a good starting point since we must always start our questioning and reasoning by looking at everything from God's perspective. This does not come naturally to us, and to do that, God will humble us, bringing us to our knees and our spiritual senses. How does God do that? He does that most effectively through the test of suffering.

A Positive Outcome

There will be times when our faith seems to have failed us because the testing of our faith appears to have got the better of us. We might condemn ourselves, seeing ourselves as failures because we do not possess a strong enough faith to sustain us. Yet a true faith can never really fail, and God will use our trials, not to condemn us, but to draw us closer to Him. He will bring to light our spiritual weaknesses and lack of faith, using our difficulties to open our spiritual eyes to see the incredible sufficiency of His eternal grace. Our shortcomings serve as an ongoing reminder of our limitations and God's extraordinary unlimited love and mercy, which more than make up for our inadequacies. Through it all, God will open up our understanding to recognize that, left to our own devices, we are hopeless and helpless to overcome our spiritual battles using our own strength or ingenuity.

We would do well to remember that our faith is not placed in faith, but in the person of Jesus Christ. We only have to look at the cross of Christ and His resurrection to see that He never fails us and has overcome the worst of the worst and the greatest of sins. In Jesus, God always provides us with hope and help, supplying a way of deliverance from this never-ending daily battle that we face as we strive to live by faith in a faithless, godless, sinful, fallen world.

The Apostle Peter denied Jesus three times and he wept. Three times the risen Jesus restored Peter's faith. If Peter's faith can fail when the time of testing comes, so can yours and so can mine. Can you imagine if God struck us off every time we failed? Such a predicament would provide us with a life of constant fear, since we know that we have the potential to fail God at any time. We would do well to remember how easy it is for any of us to let down our spiritual guard through some act of carelessness, neglect or temptation. In such cases, we must do everything we can to identify what has gone wrong and rectify it as soon as we can.

> 'If we say we have no sin, we deceive ourselves, and the truth is not in us. If we confess our sins, he is faithful and just to forgive us our sins and to cleanse us from all unrighteousness' (1 John 1:8–9).

The testing of faith proves to *us* how effective our faith is. Just as a newborn baby boy/girl is born in weakness, this does not make that baby any less a real human being. Given time, the baby will grow up into a strong, healthy adult. This growth is dependent upon first being fed milk, then weaned onto spoon-fed healthy food to the point where the baby can feed for itself. If the baby remained a baby, that would signal that something is not right because no physical growth has taken place. As a baby continues to grow into a child and their conscience kicks in, he learns to distinguish between right and wrong, learning how to apply those differences to his own life and the world around him. As growth continues, he will gain understanding, wisdom and knowledge. Through education, observation and learning from personal experience of what works well and what does not, he learns how to make informed good choices and decisions that will benefit both him and others. In this regard, I think it is true to say that we learn more from our mistakes than we do any other way.

So it is with faith. Faith may start off weak, but that does not mean a person is not a real Christian. Through being fed and nurtured by the healthy food of God's word to us in the Bible, we allow God to speak into our lives, providing us with a better understanding and a greater knowledge about the character and nature of God and our identity of who we are in Christ. Through obedience to what we learn and understand, our faith cannot fail to grow up into a mature, strong and healthy faith. As faith continues to grow and mature, God will test it to make it even stronger. While the test might be a painful experience, God's design is not to push us away from Him, but to draw us closer to Him.

When our response to the severe testing of our faith is to call God to account, we demonstrate a lack of understanding of what it means to trust in His sovereignty. Instead, we live as though our lives still belong to us and not God. We accuse God of being unreasonable and unfair. We feel hard done by, cheated, and become bitter and full of resentment. Left unchecked, we begin to spiral out of control, losing our sense of spiritual balance and eternal perspective. The remedy is not so much about removing the test, but the removal of our ownership of this life and the expectation for God to think like we do. As followers of Christ, our life is not primarily about us, our health, wealth, happiness or even our families; it is supremely about our witness and testimony to the salvation we have in Jesus. When we call God to account, we fail to comprehend or appreciate God's ownership of us, or the incredible sufficiency of His saving grace. Through all the trials of life, God is teaching us to live by faith and not by sight (2 Cor. 5:7). This is essential training that prepares us to depend on and trust in Him no matter what. It produces a tried and tested faith that is proved to be real, able to live in the real world believing in a real God who is indeed a God of love.

Is God Taking a Huge Risk When He Tests our Faith?

When God puts our faith to the test, does He run the risk of losing some of us? Might we turn against Him if we fail to endure the test? One thing is for sure; God will never drive anyone who belongs to Him away from Him. Jesus said:

> '*All that the Father gives me will come to me, and whoever comes to me I will never cast out*' (John 6:37).

For those of us who belong to God, His purpose is to strengthen our faith in Jesus and bring us to a place of greater dependency upon him. The stronger our faith, the better equipped we will be to live a life of witness in a world that is faithless. The evil of Satan cannot penetrate such faith in Christ, in fact, we use our faith to protect us from whatever Satan throws at us. Paul writes to the church in Ephesus:

> '*In all circumstances take up the shield of faith, with which you can extinguish all the flaming darts of the evil one*' (Eph. 6:16).

In His providence, God will engineer our circumstances, using different means and avenues to test us. He will even use the agency of Satan, giving him permission to do his worst. Satan always sets out to work against God, seeking to destroy a person's faith and God's credibility. Even so, God remains in complete overall control as we can see in the biblical story of Job.

Will God Test Us More than We Can Handle?

In the times of our testing, many of us would say that we cannot handle any more. There are historical records of numerous faithful Christians throughout the course of history, whose severe testing we may consider to have been beyond their ability to endure. They have been taken to the limit and beyond. I cannot find anywhere in the Bible that says God will not give us more testing than we can handle. However, in such times we can be sure that the sufficiency of God's grace will empower us to go through it. Writing to the church in Corinth, the Apostle Paul says:

> *'For we do not want you to be unaware, brothers, of the affliction we experienced in Asia. For we were so utterly burdened beyond our strength that we despaired of life itself. Indeed, we felt that we had received the sentence of death. But that was to make us rely not on ourselves but on God who raises the dead'* (2 Cor. 1:8–9).

What the Bible *does* promise us is that God will not allow us to be *tempted* beyond that which we can endure and that He will always provide a way out of the temptation:

> *'No temptation has overtaken you that is not common to man. God is faithful, and he will not let you be tempted beyond your ability, but with the temptation he will also provide the way of escape, that you may be able to endure it'* (1 Cor. 10:13).

Some Christians have endured years of severe testing, but never lived to see the day of their 'good' until after they have died and received their heavenly reward. James writes:

> *'Blessed is the man who remains steadfast under trial, for when he has stood the test he will receive the crown of life, which God has promised to those who love him'* (James 1:12).

Chapter 17

THE TESTING OF MY OWN FAITH

For two years (1992–1994), my faith was put to the test in what I call the Desert Place. It would be no exaggeration to say that this test was unbearable and incredibly tormenting. It was both brutal and pitiless in its execution, leaving me feeling totally destroyed, desolate and worthless. At the time, I did not recognize it as a test.

Today, I find my faith undergoing another severe time of testing because of cancer. Although there are significant differences between the two tests, there are many similarities. As was the case in my Desert Place, I do not know today what the future holds. While I can look back to see how God rescued me from the Desert, I do not know if He will rescue me from the trial of today. For the sake of my family and the ongoing opportunity to bear witness to my faith, I pray that God will rescue me once again. In my Desert test, God taught me how to survive by taking refuge in Him and His word, an invaluable lesson that I apply today just as I did back then.

Once again, I find myself in a position of uncertainty, having no control over what will happen to me. Does this fill me with despair? Not at all, for it reminds me how much I constantly need to live, depending upon the sovereignty of God. That is a most treasured lesson to learn and one of the purposes of all tests. I have been here before and know from experience that dependency teaches me to *trust* in God whatever may happen. I know that through the testing, God is not seeking to destroy my faith but to build it up. The Bible convinces me that God is testing my faith so that there is always going to be a positive outcome, whether that materializes in this life or the next. The testing of today is teaching me once again to depend less on myself and more on God.

Does God want me to be miserable in my suffering? No, what kind of a witness is that? Whilst I freely admit to feeling really fed up from time to time, I know that the testing of my faith serves to empower me to lay hold of the joy of my salvation and the bigger picture of my future inheritance, stored up for me in heaven. The Apostle Peter writes:

> '*In this you rejoice, though now for a little while, if necessary, you have been grieved by various trials, so that the tested genuineness of your faith—more precious than gold that perishes though it is tested by fire—may be found to result in praise and glory and honor at the revelation of Jesus Christ*' (1 Peter 1:6–7).

It seems that just prior to the second coming of Jesus, the testing of the entire world will be so great and severe, that Jesus said:

> '*When the Son of Man comes, will he find faith on earth?*' (Luke 18:8)

I have to confess that to be severely tested twice could tempt me to feel as though God is expecting too much from me. From where I stand today, I look back at the Desert and still remember its pain and sense of hopelessness. Even though I could not see it at the time, it was only later that I began to see how God brought me through that place and used it to serve His purposes. God turned that Desert curse into a place of Paradise blessing. That priceless experience has helped me to understand that God has a purpose in my current trial.

As I look back over my entire life, I can recognize five distinct seasons, three of which were places that God used to form, test and establish my faith.

Chapter 18

CHRISTIAN HERITAGE (1960–1992)

The first season that I can identify the beginnings of my faith was through my Christian upbringing. I was born in 1960 and raised in a Christian family in Chessington, Surrey. I am forever grateful to my parents, who brought me up with a Christian background into which many seeds were sown. Those seeds were slow to grow but were not without due effect. As I grew up and began to gain my independence (1977–1992), I pretty much just got on with life, doing the very best I could and making the most of what capabilities and opportunities I had.

In 1976, aged 16, I left school having just about managed to scrape through with four O levels. Apart from the boyhood dream of playing football for Chelsea or becoming a professional drummer, I had no idea about what I wanted to do in life. I enjoyed the very hot summer of 1976, lazing around before entering into full-time work later that year as a clerical assistant in the Inland Revenue, Kingston.

The plan was to start at the bottom and work my way up. After about one year, I decided that working in an office environment was not for me. I altered course and began to work alongside an older friend who was a heating service engineer. In 1980, aged 20, I put down a deposit with my fiancée to purchase our first house in Leatherhead, a two-up two-down Victorian semi, in preparation for getting it ready for married life. In 1981 while attending Kingston Christian Fellowship, we married. In about 1985, we moved from our existing house to a much larger Victorian house just around the corner. Because of its derelict state, the only other people interested in it were builders. Seeing its great potential as a sound investment, I made a closed bid at auction which proved to be successful. Apart from some major structural work, I undertook the renovation myself. Once the work was completed, and seeing the monetary profit that could be made, I acquired the taste for doing this kind of thing again in the future. Property prices were rising fast, including houses that needed a lot of work doing to them. In about 1990, we sold our home, made a decent profit, and moved to Devon where property prices were much lower. I began to work for Servowarm as a heating service engineer, covering the counties of Devon, Dorset and Somerset. We had purchased a third of an acre elevated building plot just outside Lyme Regis, which came with a mature garden together with detailed planning permission for a four-bedroom detached house and double garage. Acting as site manager, I organized its construction, and the house was completed within budget and the time frame of six months. In February 1992, we moved into our new home. Along the way, we had three daughters: Natasha in 1985, Jade in 1987 and Tiffany in 1990.

During the first 32 years of my life, my experience of church life had been wide and varied, including lengthy periods at Chessington Evangelical Church (now The King's Centre), Kingston Christian Fellowship (a charismatic house fellowship that was part of the charismatic renewal taking place at that time), St George's in Ashtead (Anglican), Kilmington Baptist and, in much later years, Bovey Baptist (both in Devon).

Throughout those years, I lived as a typical decent, good, law-abiding citizen. Even at the age of 32, the faith I possessed was one that I had largely inherited from my Christian upbringing, and I had simply stayed in that groove and never wandered off. For any Christian parents, that is a blessing in itself. I believed that when I died, I would end up in heaven and not hell. That just about summed up my faith, and it kept me going for the first 32 years of my life.

Chapter 19

THE DESERT PLACE (1992-1994)

The second distinct season that God used to develop my faith is what I call the Desert Place. This was a place which saw my faith develop through the trial of severe testing. At the age of 32, and for the first time in my life, my faith was profoundly examined. In the Desert, I found myself at rock bottom, a broken man and ready to give up on life, yet it was here that God brought me into a greater understanding and realization of what a real faith is and what a real faith looks like.

In February 1992, I was very happy and content with a life that had never before felt so satisfying or looked so promising. Little did I know that just around the corner, my world was about to come crashing down. Two weeks after moving into our newly built home, Servowarm made me redundant due to the property recession at that time. It was a case of last one in, first one out. While this was bad news and a big blow, it did not present us with any immediate financial threat since I had a mortgage protection policy in place that gave us breathing space. This was a storm that I believed would soon pass, but instead it grew much worse. After a few months, my wife told me that she was going to divorce me. Those words came as a total shock and a thunderbolt from out of the blue.

While I was more than aware that the divorce statistics had risen sharply and had now become accepted and normal within our secular society, I had never contemplated that I could become a part of that statistic. However, divorce was becoming more acceptable within Christian circles, just as gay marriage has in more recent years. Up until now, I had felt safe and secure in my marriage and family life and never saw this coming.

Losing my job was one thing, but that was always going to be replaceable. Losing everything that I had lived for and was precious to me, such as my marriage, family and the family home, could never be replaced. Even my pet cat was killed by a car! I felt as though I was losing my life, identity, sense of purpose, self-worth, self-esteem and control. As with many divorces, it was not just the sense of loss but the immense pain of rejection and abandonment that goes with it.

No matter how much I wept or how hard I tried to bring about reconciliation, the decision to divorce was already set in stone. I reasoned that to drive my wife to do something so extreme, I must have been such an awful person to live with. I begged for mercy and forgiveness. I cried out to God, begging Him to somehow step in and intervene.

The emotional torment was crippling. My world had gone so fast from living in a safe world, full of promise and expectation, to an unrecognizable world of hostility, uncertainty and destruction. Apart from my parents, I felt as though I could no longer trust anyone. I reasoned that all of the years of hard work and sacrifice to do my best were now meaningless. I saw no point in carrying on since my life no longer made any sense to me. I developed a deep empathy for those who choose to give up on life by taking their own life because they can see no other way of release from whatever agony they have to live with.

While I had always faced up to the reality that there is no such thing as a perfect Christian or a perfect marriage, I struggled to get what was taking place to add up in my head. I could understand how these things happen outside of the Christian faith, but not within it; how could a Christian divorce even be possible or make sense?

I am more than aware that this book is not the place to disclose personal details but suffice to say it was the use of Christianity to justify the divorce that was having such a profound effect on me, forcing me to question the validity of the Christian faith. I reasoned that if this was a true reflection of Christianity, then I did not want to have anything to do with it. For the first time in my life, my eyes were opened to a brand of Christianity that promoted a 'God wants me to be happy' theology, no matter what the cost.

Through all that was taking place, I could see that I was being replaced as both a husband and father, the impact of which was devastating. As a consequence, I probably became one of the biggest cynics and sceptics of the Christian faith. Having said that, I recognized that God was not responsible for how others choose to behave and never for one moment blamed God or became angry with Him. My scepticism was aimed at the Christianity that embraced and justified wrong and wilful behaviour because 'God is so full of grace and unconditional love.' No matter how hard I tried, I could not identify myself with such a God.

Against my wishes, the family home was put on the market. For the best part of the next two years, I lived alone in a friend's granny flat. Remaining unemployed, I had plenty of time to reflect on my life and how I got to be where I was. As for the future, I could not see one. I had been stripped of everything except my health. Losing all that I had lived for provoked me to question whether I could be stripped of my faith; after all, I was just about ready to quit Christianity. In what I have since believed to be the providence of God and with nothing else better to do, I decided to examine and scrutinize what the Bible had to say about the Christian faith. I took myself into the Bible and began to study it systematically from front to back, again and again, something I had never done before. Over the years, I had been brought up to know all the important aspects of the Bible and had sat under a lot of teaching, but even so, I had never studied the Bible in depth for myself but relied on others to feed me. Now I found myself coming to the Bible for myself. I wanted to study it with no preconceived ideas, as though I knew nothing and was starting from scratch. In my desperation to let the Bible speak for itself, I was determined to empty myself of everything that I thought I knew. I refrained from looking at all Christian publications since I did not want them to influence me in any way. At the heart of it all, I was determined to find out what a real faith looks like and what difference does it really make to our lives.

The Powerful Spotlight of God's Word

As I studied my Bible, it was easier to examine why the world around me was so full of everything that is evil and wrong. On the other hand, it was far more difficult to examine the Christian world around me that had led me into such confusion. I came to the Bible asking what difference does faith really make to one's life and the choices that are made? One of the really big questions I had was: does it really matter? Does it make any difference if I choose to sleep around or have an affair while claiming to be a Christian because God is so loving and forgiving?

From early childhood, I had been brought up to believe that it did matter, but my eyes were now being opened to a Christianity that was changing very fast and lived as though it doesn't really matter. This was a Christianity that knew what the ideal was yet excused itself from living up to that ideal because God knows that we are only human. It was a Christianity that claimed it doesn't really matter because 'once saved always saved.' This I found difficult to accept since it gives licence to have the best of both worlds. It gives us all the world has to offer and all the forgiveness that God has to offer. Is that possible?

A battle was taking place in my mind; perhaps I had got it all wrong and had allowed myself to cling to wrong assumptions all my life. My eyes were being opened to a Christianity that was changing with the times and culture, forcing me to examine whether I needed to change and go with the flow, or perhaps now was the time to quit Christianity and the church altogether. I found it all so terribly confusing as I questioned the validity of faith itself. I was determined to find out the answers to my

125

questions directly from the Bible. As I examined all things Christian, I inevitably found myself examining my own faith. What faith did I have? Was it real or was it a sham? I only wanted to have the real thing or none at all.

I have never been a great reader, but the more I studied the Bible for myself, the more I was drawn into it. I devoted a large portion of my empty days feeding on it. I developed an insatiable hunger for the written word of God, and it was as though the Bible had become my food. For the first time in my life, the Bible was becoming so relevant and alive as it spoke directly into my mind and circumstances. I discovered that as I read it, the Bible was reading and examining me. It challenged and rebuked me most severely, but at the same time, gave me tremendous encouragement and great hope. My prayer life took off as I prayed my way through what I was studying. For the first time in my Christian life, the Bible really meant something to me. I began to perceive God's awesome majesty and the greatness of His attributes: His character, nature, holiness, mercy, judgment, wrath, justice, love and grace. The effect of such revelation acted like a powerful searchlight that penetrated deep into my soul. At the same time, it brought to light just how far away I was from God's perfect standards and His expectations of me. As I continued to open myself up to the pages of the Bible, I not only began to recognize what a real faith looked like, but that my own faith did not match up to what Christ demanded of me.

How did I not see or understand any of this before? Unfortunately, I know that I am not the only Christian who has allowed themselves to be so distracted by life, living in ignorance of what the Bible teaches. As I continued to study the Bible, it was as though I was standing before the judgment seat of Christ who was calling me to account. All that I had been, was and should be was now being revealed. I began to discover that my Christian life did nothing but endorse a cozy, comfortable, casual faith that suited me. The more I read the Bible, the more I began to see the difference between a faith that is false and a faith that is real, a faith that is dead and a faith that is alive. I only had to look at myself to discover that the prime exhibit under examination in all of this was myself.

As I continued to study, one of the things that really hit me hard was the considerable number of warnings which call upon professing Christians to make sure that they are actually *in* the faith. For example, we are told by the Apostle Paul to test our faith for ourselves:

> *'Examine yourselves, to see whether you are in the faith. Test yourselves. Or do you not realize this about yourselves, that Jesus Christ is in you, unless indeed you fail to meet the test?'* (2 Cor. 13:5).

I began to examine my understanding of the phrase 'once saved always saved.' In my Christian life I had grown up with the mindset that I was pretty safe, believing that once someone goes through the motion of accepting Jesus into their heart, they are guaranteed salvation provided they remain a good Christian. However, in my study of the Scriptures, it became all too apparent that there are many Christians who think they are good enough to be saved, but who will get the biggest shock of their lives to hear Jesus say to them on the Day of Judgment: *'Away from me, I never knew you!'* (Matt. 7:23). It sounds like the 'many' that Jesus referred to were convinced that they knew Him, doing plenty of good things in His name, yet Jesus tells them that He *never* knew them! The shocking truth that comes from this is that not everyone who thinks they are a Christian actually are. There are many Christians who think they are 'once saved, always saved' and can never be 'unsaved', yet they have never been saved in the first place! Since I was in the process of examining my own faith, I was challenged to find out if I could lose my own salvation. Was that possible? What assurance did I have that I possessed a faith that saves me? Through the plain reading of Scripture, I concluded that there is no such thing as 'once saved always saved', or at least not in the sense that so many Christians like to believe. My understanding led me to believe that the assurance of salvation can only be realized as a person *continues* to abide in a faith that *continues* to abide in Jesus, and that this ongoing way of life *will* produce the good fruit of the Holy Spirit in a person's life, made manifest by their character and the choices they make.

Repentance

The recognition of my cozy, comfortable, casual faith brought me into a place of deep sorrow and conviction. I saw the need to repent of such superficiality and began to appreciate that repentance is not a one-off confession that marked the day I became a Christian, but rather an ongoing repentance and confession that is to be a way of life. My repentance brought me into a greater awareness of my sin and my inability to remain sin free even on my best days, no matter how hard I try. The word of God revealed the true state of my faith to be flabby, flimsy, shallow, part-time and weak, knowing more *about* Jesus than actually knowing Him as Lord of my life. I had not taken God seriously, and my priorities were devoted to other really good things, such as family and our way of life, rather than to Christ. You can imagine how the following words of Jesus struck me in a new way:

> 'Whoever *loves father or mother more than me is not worthy of me, and whoever loves son or daughter more than me is not worthy of me. And whoever does not take his cross and follow me is not worthy of me. Whoever finds his life will lose it, and whoever loses his life for my sake will find it.*' (Matt. 10:37–39).

The above verse, and many like it, thundered home that it was either all or nothing. The verdict was that I had not given Christ my all, far from it.

The Death of Self

The deserts of the world are hostile places. Water and food are hard to come by. Drop a person in the middle of a desert with no supplies or protection and they will soon die. In my Desert Place, I was put to death, not once but twice. First, I was put to death by losing everything that was precious to me, and as a result, I was ready to give up on life and die. Second, I was put to death by the word of God, which called for me to die to self and die to this world. The whole Desert experience brought me to the end of myself twice over, and I was ready to be buried in the sand.

I must hasten to add that the first putting to death left me for dead, whereas the second putting to death through the word of God brought me to life and gave me hope. The second putting to death revealed that the demonstration of a true faith necessitates the death of self in order to be raised to a new life that lives for Christ. How can anyone truly surrender themselves to Christ unless they have died to everything else? Dying to self means dying to self-interest, while dying to this world means dying to the serving and lusting after the things of this world. Surrender to God means living to serve the interests of God. This kind of surrender had never before entered my head! The faith I had lived with was one that simply tagged Christ onto the rest of the good life I had lived. At best, this was a half-hearted faith that only required me to continue living a morally good life and confess to being a Christian. In reality I was living to serve myself, which meant that Jesus was not Lord of my life, I was. I had always known, accepted and believed in all of the elementary teachings that pertain to the Christian faith, but had never positioned Jesus to be Lord of my life, through which He is my Master and I His slave. This leaves no room for self-pity; if one has died to self, how can one indulge in self-pity? Self-pity is replaced by the complete surrendering of all to Christ.

As I look back at the pain and torment of the Desert Place, I see that God made good use of it all. He brought me to my knees and to the end of myself and into a position where I was ready to abdicate everything to Christ in a way that perhaps was not possible before. In that Desert, God crushed me but did not leave me for dead. Although it might sound strange, I thank Him for doing that because if He had not, I would have carried on living as though my life belonged to me and not Christ. I saw that a life of true faith is a life that completely belongs to Christ and lives to do His will. God had brought me to the place where I was ready to give up completely, handing over ownership of my mind, body and soul to Him. In bringing me to the end of myself and the death of 'me', God brought me into a greater understanding of what took place at the cross. The wreck I had become through the complete obliteration of all self-esteem was replaced by the sufficiency of who I am in Christ. At the cross, I died with Christ, and through His resurrection, I am raised to a new life that lives *in* Him. Jesus is my life, and the astonishing thing is that, by His Spirit, He lives in me. This is what it means to be united with Christ in His life, death, resurrection and glorification.

Dependency Upon the Word of God

If God had decided to end my life in that Desert and take me home to be where He is, I would have welcomed it with arms wide open. Yet God did not do that; instead He brought me close to Him by speaking to me through His word. The Desert Place brought me into a reliance upon God and His word that I had not experienced before, creating an ongoing desire to seek God through the study of my Bible, combined with prayer. Since God has chosen to use the Bible as His primary way to reveal Himself to us, I can vouch from personal experience that the Bible is a priceless book. Through it, God has revealed the knowledge of Himself and His salvation found only in Jesus. Throughout the Bible, God instructs and teaches disciples of Jesus how to live a life of genuine, authentic faith in Him, a faith that makes a difference to our mindset and the way in which we live our lives.

Faith Lives in the Sufficiency of God's Grace

One of the aspects of the Christian faith that really came alive for me in the Desert Place is the centrality of the cross of Jesus and its dominant significance. Because of my execution in the Desert, the suffering and death of Christ on a cross became all the more elaborate to me. Even though I do not deserve it, God demonstrated His love for me by choosing to save me from myself and the condemnation of my sin. God chose the means of the cross to do this, and Jesus chose to obey God His Father by going through with it. What a cost! What surrender! What obedience to the call of dreadful suffering! What a sacrifice! What humility! What a Servant! What grace! What mercy! In the Desert, the very place of condemnation and rejection, I gained a profound indebtedness to God's forgiveness, acceptance and undeserved mercy. This gave me a renewed sense of worth and purpose. For the first time in my Christian life, I had ears to hear what God was speaking to me and my eyes were opened to see, not only the immensity of God's saving grace, but what God's grace demanded of me. For the first time, I understood that Jesus purchased my life for Himself at the cross. For the first time, I gained an authentic love for God, both for who He is and what He has done for me. I was beginning to recognize that a real faith is the faith that lives in *response* to what Jesus accomplished at the cross and whose sacrifice there is sufficient for all time and in all circumstances, providing me with sufficient forgiveness, justification, righteousness, mercy, security, peace and hope for the future. The day I stand before Jesus is an awesome prospect, for I will see my salvation face to Face.

The Cross of Christ Comes to Life

Sufficient not only means plenty, it can also mean enough and adequate. The sufficiency of God's grace speaks so powerfully of the finished work of Jesus at the cross, because it was adequate enough to free me from my sin and make me right with God. What Jesus accomplished at the cross is so phenomenal to the point of being foolishly unbelievable and ridiculous. What sane person would ever believe such an astonishing story, especially in today's sceptical society? Jesus took Himself to the cross, sacrificing His life for me, taking upon Himself the wrath and judgment of a Holy God that in my unworthiness, I rightly deserved. Perhaps the most profound truth that the cross demonstrates to me is that God is for me, not against me. At the cross, Jesus took upon Himself my Judgment Day so that I would not have to. The Apostle John wrote:

> '*For God so loved the world, that he gave his only Son, that whoever believes in him should not perish but have eternal life. For God did not send his Son into the world to condemn the world, but in order that the world might be saved through him. Whoever believes in him is not condemned, but whoever does not believe is condemned already, because he has not believed in the name of the only Son of God*' (John 3:16–18).

In the Desert Place, I had come to the end of myself and was ready to give up on life; I'd had enough. Being put to death in this way helped me to understand more clearly what it means to be crucified with Christ and His call to deny myself, pick up my cross and follow Him. The Desert proved to be a place of both death and resurrection, and it was there that God met with me and gave to me what I really needed in life. Even though I could not see it or feel it, His deliverance was always with me. He put me to death by breaking me and then rescued me, providing me with spiritual food and drink that raised me back to a life that was better equipped to serve and live for Him and His interests.

Faith Forgives

I do not think that God would have allowed me to move on from the Desert until I learnt a most fundamental characteristic of the Christian faith: the command by Jesus to forgive others. In light of the fact that Jesus obtained the forgiveness of my own sins against God, how could I justify myself by holding anything against those who have wronged me? One knows whether one has forgiven others when one finds themselves praying for their salvation and for them to be made right with God. I am satisfied that on the Day of Judgment, we will all be held accountable to God as individuals. Faith is personal and so too is God's judgment. On that Day, no one will be held accountable to me but to God, and I too will be held accountable to God and no one else.

New Identity and Purpose

The Desert Place was a two-year experience of solitude with God where I learned to take refuge in Him. Having been put to death, I re-emerged back into the world with a new identity and a new sense of purpose. Even though I had no idea what the future held, I came out with the conviction and passion that there is only one way that makes sense of living this precious gift of life in a fallen world. That way is to live life in order to serve God, by loving Him with all of my heart, mind, soul and strength. Such a life necessitates a faith that is real and alive. I also came out with a sense of the prophetic, that there were tough times ahead for the church in this country. Everything was going to be shaken and God was the one who was going to do it. Along with this warning came a strong awareness of the necessity for the church to wake up, grow up and love God with all. Spending time alone with God in the isolation of the Desert Place gave to me a tremendous awareness of my necessity to rely and depend upon Him at all times. I had lost everything except my faith which had forced me to examine what I am left with once everything I own and have achieved is taken away. This is precisely what will happen on the day of my physical death when my soul is separated from my body. On that day, I will not need food, drink, clothes, or any of the basic necessities of life or even the air that I breathe. While all these things are integral to everyday life, none of those things will serve any more purpose or hold any value. Everything that I need on the day of my death will be found in Jesus, and He will mean everything to me on that day. The truth is, Jesus means everything to me while I am still alive in the body, knowing that if I know Jesus, I have everything that I *really* need.

After about two years, God took me out of the Desert and led me into the places of physical renewal and physical restoration.

Chapter 20

THE PLACE OF RENEWAL (1994–1997)

The third season God used to shape my faith was in the Place of Renewal. It was to be a place of great blessing. While in the Desert Place, I recognized that my role as both husband and father was being taken away from me and given to another. I was not content to let this happen without taking a stand, so I applied for custody of my three daughters, but in March 1994, I learned that my application was not successful. Armed with this news, I decided that I needed to get far away for a while. I contacted a Christian holiday company and offered my services, telling them that I would do anything that they offered me. Because I was very practical with my hands, they offered me the position of hotel handyman at their resort in Kefalos on the Greek island of Kos.

In April 1994, I travelled out to Kos and found myself sharing a cockroach-infested basement room with two teenage fellow workers. This was a far cry from what I was accustomed to back in England. Nevertheless, I settled down to my new way of life, making lots of new friends and having some really great times. The hotel offered water sports for the guests, and I spent every spare moment learning how to windsurf. As the season wore on, the waterfront manager saw my rapid progress and suggested I came back the following summer season to work as a watersports instructor. In November, I returned to my parents in England on the Sussex coast to obtain my RYA qualifications as a windsurfing and sailing instructor, together with a powerboat licence for rescue purposes. I returned to Kos in April 95 and enjoyed an incredible season doing something that I had never thought possible. I hadn't planned any of this but received it all as God's incredible gracious provision and blessing.

The 1995 summer season ended in November, and I signed up for another summer season starting in April 1996. While staying with my parents during the winter, I was surprised to be asked by the same holiday company if I could go out to the French Alps to replace a ski guide/technician who had returned home early. Although I felt daunted by the fact that I only had two weeks skiing experience under my feet, I did not hesitate to accept and rise to the challenge! In January1996, I arrived in the French ski resort of Alpe d'Huez and was given one week to find my way around the mountains and discover my ski feet before the guiding of guests began. I remember my arrival at the resort very clearly. As I drove up the hairpin road that leads from the valley below up to the ski resort, I looked around at the imposing grandeur of the snow-filled mountain range. With a touch of fear and trepidation, I wondered about the challenges that lay ahead. I recall my arrival at the chalet, where I met the rest of the small team of staff. I especially remember one of the staff who worked as a chalet girl. We shook hands as she greeted me with the words, 'Hi, I'm Krissie.'

As the season went by, I remember thinking that Krissie would make a wonderful wife for someone, never thinking that someone could be me. I had nothing to offer her, so what could she possibly see in me? I was a reject who had no money, no prospects, no status and no nothing. On the other hand, Krissie was fresh out of Cambridge University, was 10 years younger than I and had so much going for her. Besides, I had vowed never to allow myself to get involved in another relationship for fear of exposing myself to the same vulnerability that I had previously experienced.

We were soon spending our spare time together on the slopes. However, in March 96, Krissie unexpectedly returned to England following the premature death of her mother. This left me thinking that I would probably never see her again.

The ski season ended in early April 1996. I returned to my parent's home in the UK for a quick turn-around before leaving for the summer season in Kos in late April. To my great delight, Krissie successfully applied for the job of children's worker at the same hotel where I was based. She was due to come out in June, and I drove to Kos airport to meet her. I waited for what seemed to be a very long time, staring intently into the sky, willing her aircraft to appear on the distant horizon as it made its descent. At last, it came into view and taxied toward the terminal. I watched the passengers disembark on the runway till there were no more left, but there was no sign of Krissie. My heart sank as I reasoned that she must have changed her mind. I went back to the hotel with heavy shoulders, but when I arrived, I was informed that she had simply missed her flight. A huge spring returned to my step, and to my relief and joy, she managed to catch the next plane out.

We worked the rest of the 1996 season, devoting our spare time together. As a result, I did not get to spend much spare time on the water windsurfing, but it was a great place to be romancing. It was obvious by the end of the season that our relationship was going somewhere. I remember thinking that the impossible was beginning to take place. This was ridiculous. Here was a beautiful young lady, who by her own choice appeared as though she might possibly entertain the idea of taking our relationship further. I remember feeling how incredible it was to feel accepted and no longer rejected.

At the end of the summer season in November, I returned back to my parents on the south coast while Krissie returned to her mother's house in North London. We both decided not to work the winter season so that we could test our relationship to see if it would stand up to the test of normal, mundane everyday life back in England. Krissie took to work as a primary school teacher, while I looked to see if I could slip back into the heating service industry near to where she lived. This was a period that gave me the opportunity to work out where God was in all of this. In the Place of Renewal, God had brought many blessings my way that I had never thought possible just a few years earlier. I did not search for these blessings; they simply came my way, and I took hold of the opportunities presented to me. I recognized that the blessings I had enjoyed in that place came from the hand of God as He continued to lead and guide me. For obvious reasons, Krissie was the greatest and most significant blessing of them all.

Remarriage?

While we continued to test our relationship, I began to seriously address the whole issue of remarriage, something I had not had to do before. During my study in the Desert on what the Bible had to say about divorce, I was more than aware of the words of Jesus:

'And I say to you: whoever divorces his wife, except for sexual immorality, and marries another commits adultery' (Matt. 19:9).

'You shall not commit adultery' (Exod. 20:14).

In the Gospel of Matthew, Jesus took the whole concept of committing adultery to a whole new level. He said:

'You have heard that it was said "You shall not commit adultery." But I tell you, everyone who looks at a woman with lustful intent has already committed adultery with her in his heart' (Matt. 5:27–28).

The Apostle Paul writes:

'Or do you not know that the unrighteousness will not inherit the kingdom of God? Do not be deceived: neither the sexually immoral, nor idolaters, nor adulterers, nor men who practice homosexuality, nor thieves, nor the greedy, nor drunkards, nor revilers, nor swindlers will inherit the kingdom of God' (1 Cor. 6:9–10).

Included in the list of people who will not inherit the kingdom of God is the one who commits adultery. As somebody who had been divorced by another who had since remarried, was I now free to remarry? Remarriage in the eyes of the law of the land is not only legal and accepted but common practice. Nonetheless, if I was to marry Krissie, would I be entering into a union that God did not recognize and who viewed such a thing as legalised adultery?

I searched the Scriptures, desperate not to read into them what I wanted them to say. When I tried to save my previous marriage, I became well aware of the numerous Christian books and literature that said while it was not God's ideal, it was okay to get divorced *and* remarry; but was this true? Even if that was the case, I didn't want to do something that was just okay with God. I needed to know whether it was right or wrong since I knew that I could not expect God to bless something if it was the wrong thing to do. I knew it was more important to obtain happiness by living in obedience to God and that I could never be happy while knowingly living in disobedience to God. I understood that true happiness rested in obedience to God, and I did not want to do anything that would jeopardize that rest or throw it away. After much study and agonizing prayer, I concluded from reading Scripture in its plainest sense that I was free to remarry. The Bible verse that carried so much weight for me was Matthew 19:9:

'Whoever divorces his wife, except for sexual immorality, and marries another commits adultery.'

The above verse uttered by Jesus implies that if the instigator of the divorce is committing sexual immorality (fornication), then the innocent person is free to remarry. My conclusion was based upon the fact that I was not the one who initiated the divorce and had fought for reconciliation to take place, taking every opportunity to state in the legal proceedings that I was not in favour of the divorce. Before I went out to Kos to work my first season, I concluded that the day my wife married someone else was the day of no turning back, signalling the actual death blow to our marriage. That day came and went in the early summer of

1994. In February 1997, Krissie chose an engagement ring, and all I had to do was order it. I struggled over this decision, not because I believed it was wrong for me to remarry, but because I was desperate to know for certain that this was what God wanted for us both. In the Place of Renewal, God blessed me so much, and I did not want to do anything to step outside of His blessing and protection. I needed to have no doubts whatsoever and be completely sure that God was at the very centre, blessing it all. I know that we should never put God to the test or place conditions upon Him, but on this occasion, I must have come very close! I prayed fervently that if God did not want us to get married, He would make that very clear to me. I forced the situation by setting a future day and time of about four weeks hence on which I was to go ahead and order the ring. I prayed that if it was not God's will for us to get married, He would step in and intervene by initiating a phone call from Masterski before the set deadline date. I prayed this call would come in the form of a request for me to go out to France to ski guide as soon as possible. This was highly unlikely because Masterski had already employed a ski guide for the whole season. Nevertheless, with three more months of the ski season to run, I had no doubts that this was well within God's sovereignty to perform if He so willed.

I set the date and time on which to order the ring. My parents lived right on the beach at Elmer Sands on the south coast, which gave me plenty of opportunity to take long prayer walks along that beach. With only seagulls listening in, I prayed out loud for God to guide me and establish His will. The set date and time of 2pm arrived. I had given God at least one month to step in and intervene but there had been no intervention. I concluded that this was God's answer to my petition, and that it must therefore be His will for me to go ahead and order the ring. At 2pm I ordered the ring.

Two hours later, and while I was still thinking about the significance of what I had just done, the phone rang. It was

140

Masterski, informing me that their ski guide had to unexpectedly return home, and so could I step in to ski guide as soon as possible for the rest of the season. Since I was free to go, I accepted the request and the phone call ended. I remember sitting by the phone, staring at it and asking myself: Why did that phone call come when it did and not sooner? Why did it come at all? What was the point of that call coming when it did? If the call had come just three hours earlier, I would not have ordered the ring. As I continued to ponder over this, I reasoned that the timing of the call was God's way of telling me that He had indeed heard all of my prayers, and that He held back the call as a way of confirming that He was in control while leaving me in no doubt that it *was* His will for us to get married.

Chapter 21

THE PLACE OF RESTORATION (1997–2010)

The fourth season that God used to shape my faith was the Place of Restoration. The Place of Renewal was a place of physical renewal which came to an end in April 1997, paving the way for the Place of Restoration, a place that restored the things I had previously lost in the Desert Place. The Place of Restoration was to be the happiest place of my entire life. This was a place I had never expected to inhabit again. In this place, the blessings of God not only continued but increased in their significance and meaning. The pinnacle of all the blessings that God had blessed me with since leaving the Desert Place was His provision to me in the form of Krissie. For obvious reasons, she has always been the greatest earthly blessing.

The ski season in France ended in April 1997. That very same month, we married in Kenya. It rained on our wedding day, but the locals told us that rain in Africa is a sign of God's blessing, so we were happy with that. When we returned to England, I moved into Krissie's house, which had belonged to her mother. I looked for local work as a heating service engineer but also contacted my previous employer in Devon who had made me redundant back in February 1992. They were pleased to get my call, telling me of their attempts to locate my whereabouts because they wanted to offer me back my old job. Since Krissie's mother's house needed to be sold to release the inheritance to her two sisters, she was eager to make the move to Devon and get away from London. In the early winter of 1997, we moved to South Dartmoor and into our new home. The house was already called Phoenix Cottage, and in Greek mythology a phoenix was a long-lived bird that was cyclically regenerated or reborn. Associated with the sun, the phoenix obtains new life by arising from the ashes of its predecessor. It was only after purchasing the cottage that I discovered the meaning of phoenix. Although I do not adhere to Greek mythology, it seemed an appropriate name for our new home. In August 1998, Krissie gave birth to our daughter Lucy.

In May 2001, Krissie gave birth to our son James. In this Place of Restoration, God restored to me all that I had previously lost. He restored to me my beautiful wife, children, family home and my previous job covering the same areas as before. We enjoyed 13 delightful happy years living in Devon and Phoenix Cottage until the time came when we moved back London way in 2010.

As I look back upon all those four places with eyes of faith, I see the hand of God in it all. Through those places, He called me, disciplined me, broke me, put me back together, taught me, strengthened me, rescued me, blessed me, led me, guided me, provided for me, renewed and restored me. This was through no cleverness of my own but an unmerited demonstration of God's favour, grace, love and sovereignty.

Chapter 22

A STEP OF FAITH, TRUST AND OBEDIENCE

We so enjoyed living in Devon and it really was the happiest time of our lives. The natural beauty of Devon was right on our doorstep: beautiful countryside, rugged moors, stunning coastlines, all of which presented themselves as a great way to enjoy the fresh air of outdoor life. While there, we eventually settled in to our local Baptist church in Bovey Tracey. I became involved in church life as a home-group leader, worship leader, deacon, PA operator and placed on the preaching rota. My greatest passion lay in the area of preaching and teaching, since it was the power of God's word that had such a powerful impact on my own life during my Desert Place. Even so, I deeply sensed that I was not serving God in the way I ought to be. I wanted to do more but I didn't know what. I began to question whether I should push at the door of full-time ministry, but the more I did, the more I understood the significant impact this would have on the lifestyle we so enjoyed. God had brought me into the Place of Restoration in which we were relaxed and happy. It would be so much easier to stay as we were, and the last thing I wanted to do was disturb the blessings that God had given to us as a family.

However, the compelling urge to serve God in some other capacity was too strong to ignore. I tried many times to bury and overlook this sense of calling, hoping that it might fade away so that we could carry on with the life we had become comfortable with. I have to confess that at times I became frustrated by the refusal of this call to go away, and, after much prayer, I decided to reluctantly push at the door of entering into full-time ministry.

At the age of 47, and with the full support of our home church, I began to push at the door of Bristol Baptist College, making my way through the various interview and recognition procedures. I prayed at every turn that God would shut just one door if this was not His will. As it was, all the doors remained open, and the college accepted me. As we both pondered what the future held, Krissie suggested that perhaps we should go into some kind of mission-based work abroad. Yet one thing I knew for certain was that God was calling me to serve Him in the church in the United Kingdom. Ever since the time of my Desert Place, I had continued to observe the Christianity in England, recognizing the challenge that the church was already facing and was going to face on an escalating scale in the future. With this in mind, we both decided that the way forward was for me to enter into full-time ministry as a pastor.

The time came for me to hand in my notice and leave my trade. Being a family man, the thought of leaving my family and going to Bristol Baptist College for most of the week for three years did not fill me with delight. I am not an academic or intellectual and knew that at the age of 47, college was going to pose quite a challenge, but the only way for me to become a pastor was by going through college in order to gain accreditation.

I started college in September 2007 and everything about our normal way of life as a family began to disappear. I travelled up to college early Tuesday mornings and returned late Friday afternoons. We had lost my wage and the whole college experience was going to be very costly. We did our sums and worked out the finances but were not quite sure how we were going to make it all add up. Fortunately, we had managed to pay off our mortgage and, to help with our finances, Krissie worked as an assistant teacher in a local primary school, I applied for a student loan and our sending church gave us some financial help.

We both committed ourselves to what I believed God was calling me to. In my reluctance to go through with this huge change to our way of life, I saw this as an act of faith, trust and obedience. This was not Krissie's calling, and she no doubt had enormous reservations, yet she faithfully stood by me and supported me every step of the way.

Theological College

Although I believe that water baptism by full immersion is only for those who know exactly what they are doing and why, I do not label myself as a Baptist or anything else. I am simply a follower of Jesus Christ who has been called to serve Him in His church. Since I was in attendance at a Baptist college, my future ministerial role was likely to take place within the Baptist Union of churches. Even once I had finished my three years at college, there was no guarantee that any Baptist church would wish to call someone who was 50 years old, previously divorced, fresh out of college and with no previous ministerial experience. I did not relish the prospect of becoming a mature student. I had never been studious and could not see myself accomplishing the necessary theological degree. Underpinning all of my doubts was my resentment at having to spend so much time away from my family, knowing the disruption that would be imposed upon our family life. Needless to say, Krissie hated the whole experience of having to hold down a job and do family life during the week on her own. We both had to accept that I needed to go to college in order to acquire the accreditation of the Baptist Union, yet I also understood that what really counted was the recognition of God. I recalled many times that Jesus could have chosen 12 fully qualified 'Nicodemus' men to follow Him as His disciples but He did not; He chose 12 ordinary men who were mostly fishermen and who never went to college (although as Jews, they no doubt knew their Hebrew Scriptures inside out).

As I pondered upon these things, I could not help but recognize how this reliance on academic qualifications has led to the professionalization of the established church. Attending full-time college for three years to obtain a degree in theology and undergo ministerial formation didn't sit well with me; nevertheless,

I knuckled down and concentrated on getting my BA Hons degree in Theology (2/1).

I had never desired to become a vicar, minister, pastor, man of the cloth or whatever. I am just an ordinary nobody whose has responded to the call of God upon my life. In my opinion, it was my learning in the Desert Place that has properly and adequately qualified and prepared me for ministry. It was there that God set me apart, bringing me into a place of tremendous revelation, refinement and transformation. It was the Desert where God planted a call in my heart that would refuse to go away. It was there that God put me to death and stripped me of all self-reliance and self-confidence so that I might become entirely dependent upon God in ministry. Whatever the merits of theological college might be, it could not teach me what the Desert Place taught me.

Call to WBC

During my final year at college in 2009, the search for a church in need of a pastor began. They call this the period of settlement, which is far from settling. One thing I was sure of was that God was going to call me to a church that needed to wake up, grow up and commit to live in obedience to the first and greatest commandment; to love the Lord your God with all of the heart, mind, soul and strength (Mark 12:28–34). During this year, a lady from our church in Bovey shared a word that she felt was relevant to our situation. She said that while she was praying, she began to pray for us. She sensed that God was telling her that I would find a placement and that it would all happen very quickly. The month of October came to her mind, but so did January. Since the latter confused her, she did not intend to pass that part on to us, but she did.

In August 2009, I met for talks with Woodmansterne Baptist Church, which sits on the outskirts of London on the Surrey border. Having escaped to Devon in 1997, neither myself nor Krissie had ever envisaged moving back towards London. A move back

London way was not on our priority list, to say the least, and we could not bring ourselves to make such a move unless we knew for sure that this was where God wanted us to be. We visited WBC again in September for a final opportunity to take a look at the church, and they us. I specifically remember telling the church about the commission that I came with; that there were tough times ahead for the church, and that God Himself was going to shake everything, which demanded that the church spiritually wake up, grow up and love Him with all. As you can imagine, we diligently sought God's guidance. This was one of those moments when we wanted the unmistakable, clear instruction of an audible voice thundering down from heaven telling us which way to go. Instead of the thundering voice, we entrusted ourselves to the voice of God speaking through WBC's church member's meeting. They voted in favour to call me as their minister, and I duly accepted.

It was agreed that we were to move from Devon during the Christmas holiday period so that I could start ministry at the beginning of the New Year in January 2010. We began to sort out the practical details, including schools for Lucy and James. We managed to sort out James, but Lucy was not so straightforward. They were both coming from a school which had an outstanding reputation, and so we did not want their new schools to be anything less. We tried to get Lucy into one such school, St Bede's, but they had no spaces and told us that it was most unlikely for one to appear at such a late stage. October kicked in and we were still living in Devon. Out of the blue, St Bede's phoned to say that a space had become available for Lucy. This was excellent news, but the downside was that Lucy had to take up her place in time to start the new term in just two weeks' time. With no other options available, we only had two weeks to organize a very quick move from Devon to London. We arrived in Woodmansterne in October 2009, and I started ministry in January 2010. In the timing of these events, I remembered the words that the lady from our sending church had shared with us, which seemed to confirm that we were acting in accordance with the will of God.

As I have looked back over the previous 18 years, I am determined to recognize the hand of God that had brought me to where I am now. Some people might say that I am simply reading the hand of God back into past events. However, I have learnt from experience that while faith always looks forward to what is unseen, the outcome of faith can be seen in the things that have already taken place. Someone has said, 'If you want to know what will happen in the future, look back at the past.'

Leaving our home and way of life in Devon was the hardest thing for us to do. We left behind Devonshire countryside, coastlines and the smell of fresh air and farms, all of which were a part of everyday life. In Devon, we lived in a very peaceful, rural country lane, used only by horses and the odd tractor. Making the transition to living in a suburban street was a difficult concept for us both to grasp. Leaving what we knew and loved meant leaving what was normal and safe, taking a step into the unknown and unfamiliar territory. Even so, it was not a question of what *we* wanted to do, but a question of obedience to God.

Faith Always Works

The Death of a Believer

Part Three

FAITH, MINISTRY AND HEALING

Chapter 23

THE PLACE OF MINISTRY (2010–2021)

The fifth distinct season that shaped my faith was a season that called for me to put everything that I had learned about faith into full-time ministry within the church. It goes without saying that every disciple of Jesus is in full-time ministry as they live out their testimony of salvation in their everyday lives, but some are called and ordained into a particular office that serves the church in a full-time capacity.

I had often wondered why God did not lead me from the Desert Place straight into the Place of Ministry; after all, it was the Desert that had prepared me for the Place of Ministry. A total of 16 years were to pass before God led me to become the pastor of a church. Throughout those years, God demonstrated His ability to bring things out of nowhere and out of nothing, performing the unexpected and the seemingly impossible. While those 16 years proved to be a time of tremendous blessings, I believe they were a test in themselves, a test to see that I had not laid aside the valuable lessons I had learnt while in the Desert Place.

When times are good and we benefit from God's many blessings, it is very easy to relegate God to a less important place and take Him for granted. In Deuteronomy 7-8, Moses reminds the Israelites that God rescued them from a hopeless situation of bondage to Egyptian slavery and the trials of the hostile wilderness. He warned the Israelites not to forget the Lord their God after He has led them into a good land of their own, a land in which He blesses them with a rich abundance of prosperity and peace. I believe God used my 16 years of blessed renewal and restoration to teach me that I was not to forget Him but remain just as dependent upon Him as if I were still in the Desert. A few years ago, a church member at Woodmansterne asked me if I still had sand in my eyes. I think she was asking me if my Desert experience was holding me back so that I was unable to move on. I confidently told her that I moved on many years ago and resolved never to forget what God taught me in the Desert and to remember everything that I learnt to help equip, prepare and sustain me for ministry. I will always carry the Desert Place with me.

Chapter 24

UNCHARTED TERRITORY

In January 2010, I became the pastor of a real church with real people. That meant I had to become a real pastor. What did that mean? I had been thrown in at the deep end since this was all new territory for me. I was convinced that God had called me here and why but was not so sure what He was calling me into. My confidence was not high, and I felt way out of my depth, thinking that the honeymoon period would soon be over, and the church would ask for a proper pastor to step in. I now bore the title Reverend, a label I was not comfortable with since I am no more reverend than anyone else. Working as a heating engineer, customers often answered their door to me, shouting out to whoever was inside, 'It's the boiler man,' a title I felt far more comfortable with. The greatest theologian, Jesus, was not into titles. He said:

> 'But you are not to be called rabbi, for you have one teacher, and you are all brothers. And call no man your father on earth, for you have one Father, who is in heaven. Neither be called instructors, for you have one instructor, the Christ. The greatest among you shall be your servant. Whoever exalts himself will be humbled, and whoever humbles himself will be exalted' (Matt. 23:8–12).

WBC is tucked away down a quiet side street. It is out of sight and mind except to those locals who pass by every day on their way to somewhere else. The church sanctuary was built in 1936, with additional buildings added on during the 1960s and 1970s, including a sports hall, classrooms, kitchen and lounge. These later additions reflected the church's glory years when she enjoyed a time of flourishing numbers and activity. When

I arrived, those glory years were already a thing of the past, yet from the very beginning, I had high expectations for WBC. I expected God to bless her with His empowering presence that bore witness to how glorious and significant He is. I believed that God would use WBC as an example of how He can use the ordinary to bring about the extraordinary, providing her with a powerful witness to her own transformation into a church that was waking up and growing up with a determination to love God with all of her heart, mind, soul and strength. Of course, every new pastor of any church has high aspirations of what they hope to achieve, and mine totally relied upon the presence of God ministering through me. I knew from the outset that without the presence of God, I could achieve nothing. No amount of clever planning was going to bring the church into the place that she needed to be. In myself, I had nothing to offer; I do not have a magnetic, charismatic personality or crave the limelight. Neither am I a comedian or entertainer. I do not possess the marketing mindset of someone from the business world. I am not an intellectual or an academic, so, as you can see, I could not offer what a lot of churches probably look for in the pastors of today. I see myself as ordinary and unremarkable, yet I know that what matters most is not the presence of the pastor but the presence of God.

What's the Plan?

During my first six months, I gave myself time to experience the life of the church and discover who she was and what made her tick. I wanted to find out where she had come from, where she was now and how she got to be there. In this way, I set out to gauge her spiritual temperature, as well as her spiritual expectations.

The church profile stated that there were approximately 75 members, with a further 23 who attended regularly. She appeared to be a well-organized church and I soon had people on the leadership team asking me, 'What's the plan, what's the vision?' This made me begin to feel as though I was expected to run the church as though she were some kind of business corporation, the very thing I knew God had not called me to do. The only *vision* I could present to the church was Jesus, and the only *plan* I could present was the plan to love God with all of the heart, mind, soul and strength. This was not a 5-year plan but a lifetime plan. As for the vision of Jesus, that never changes! Surely there can be no better plan and vision for any church? I believe that the reason churches insist on coming up with a new plan and a new vision is because they get bored with the original plan and want something new and exciting. Of course, it is through the preaching of God's word and His whole counsel that the vision and plan are laid out for all to understand and respond to, which is to live out our salvation and testimony in the world in which we live! This response is quite simple but costly.

There is much I could say about what I learnt in my first five years of ministry, but that is not the purpose of this book. Suffice to say that I approached ministry with a mindset that leant on my past experiences, including that of working as a heating service engineer. In that role I was trained to fix things, spending much of my day dealing with unhappy customers whose heating or hot water system had broken down. My responsibility was to identify the cause of the problem, work out how to fix it and then fix and test it so that the system functioned properly and was restored to do what it was designed to do. The end goal was to make the customer happy and satisfied, winning over their confidence to use my services in the future. Using this analogy, I saw my role as a pastor as being that of a church service engineer. No newly commissioned pastor can presume anything about the church under his care. I knew that God had not called me to maintain the status quo. I knew where to start preaching, and so for about 30 weeks, my sermons focused on how a Christian's faith is properly birthed. This examined how the doctrines of justification, righteousness, sanctification and glorification all fit into the big picture. By doing this, I hoped to address misconceptions that anyone might have about what a real faith is and what it looks like. I undertook this necessary examination, not to condemn but to exhort and instruct directly from the written word of God. A key concern of mine was to get the church to understand the importance of studying the Bible for themselves. Tragically, there are so many Christians who do not see the point in studying their Bibles because they see no real need now that they have already been 'saved'. In a similar fashion, many congregations are happy to rely upon being spoon-fed the Bible through sermons or talks by others. However, unless a person can check out for themselves what is being said by going to the Scriptures for themselves, they dare not rely on a preacher who merely espouses their own opinion, backed up by a few Scriptures taken out of context! Knowing the written word of God for ourselves protects each one of us from spiritual deception, as we learn to discern what is truth and what is error:

'All Scripture is breathed out by God and profitable for teaching, for reproof, for correction, and for training in righteousness, that the man of God may be complete, equipped for every good work.' (2 Tim. 3:16)

Chapter 25

WHAT KIND OF A PASTOR?

I have already mentioned how my past experience as a heating engineer was going to help me understand my role as the pastor of a church. In addition, there were two other past experiences which I gained in the Place of Renewal that would help me understand my role. These were the times where I found myself working as a windsurfing/sailing instructor on the Greek island of Kos and as a ski guide in the French Alps.

As a ski guide, I led people through mountainous, snow-filled terrain. I was not allowed to guide skiers off-piste, which can be dangerous territory where unforeseen cliff edges and avalanches abound. The rule was to stick to the pistes, which varied from easy to difficult. On any given guide, I pointed out a distant mountain, using it as a visual marker that revealed to the group what we were aiming for and how we were going to get there. Having made the way clear, I then led the way and everyone, all of whom had differing skiing abilities, followed me. Most days, the weather was glorious, with clear deep blue skies through which the brightness of the sun's rays bounced back from the brilliance of the white snow beneath. On some days, we might find ourselves in the clouds in what is called a white-out. In such conditions, everything above you, beneath you and around you is white, producing a sense of disorientation and lostness. In these conditions, the group kept close to me since I knew the way off the piste. In the same manner, my leadership as pastor is to make the way clear and lead, armed not with a piste map but a Bible. In my leading, I stick to the Bible and aim only for Christ. In this way, I lead by example.

I came into ministry knowing that a significant aspect to my leadership lay in the area of preaching and teaching. In some ways, this is similar to the responsibility I had when I worked as a windsurfing and sailing instructor. Windsurfing was my number one sport, and I got a tremendous buzz zipping along as fast as possible on flat water in strong winds. It is possible to achieve speeds of at least 50mph in the right conditions, producing an exhilarating feeling that is driven solely by the wind and without the interference of a noisy engine. Occasionally, while speeding as fast as I could, I made a slight mistake in my body stance, instantly losing control which resulted in an unavoidable wipe-out! Since water is a soft substance, this was no real problem, and in order to recover, all that I needed to do was regain my composure, water-start and get back into the swing of things.

Sailing was my second preference, especially catamarans which, because of their twin hulls, also move along through flat water at a fast pace. One exercise I liked to do was to see how far up I could raise the hull I sat on out of the water to the craft's tipping point, holding it there for as long as possible. This can only be achieved when steering the craft hard into the wind, at which point all speed is lost, and the challenge is to maintain a constant balance between catching enough wind in the sail, holding the boat steady while using my body weight and position to maintain the boat's angle and stability. It only took a sudden, unexpected powerful gust of strong wind, together with my failure to react fast enough to depower the sail, that a capsize was inevitable. Nevertheless, having to right the craft was all part of the sailing experience.

Windsurfing and sailing boats both require the same understanding of how to position the sail in order to catch the wind. Catching the wind in the sail generates a resisting force that produces power that travels down the mast and into the hull, creating a thrust that drives the board or craft forward. If the wind is not caught in the sail in the right way, no resistance or power is generated, and the board or craft is going to remain static and unable to move forward. When the sail on a sailboat is not positioned to catch a strong wind, it flaps about vigorously and simply produces a lot of noise. In this event, the sail looks as if it's very much alive, both visually and audibly, yet it is achieving nothing. Adjusting the sail to catch the wind causes the sail to lose its flap, quieten down and generate the power needed to drive the boat forward. The result is dramatic, turning a noisy static boat into one that silently glides along the surface of the water and does what it is designed to do: sail. The more the sail is filled with the wind, the faster the boat will move forward. The stronger the wind, the more power can be transmitted through the boat to generate even more thrust. It goes without saying; if there is no wind present, then no sailing can ever take place.

Teaching people the theory of sailing has helped me to understand the goal of preaching the word of God. The theory of sailing begins on the dry beach at the water's edge. Having understood the theory, it is then put into practice on the open water. Needless to say, the more time spent on the water, putting the theory into practice and learning from mistakes, the more skilful the sailor becomes in their ability to sail in all kinds of weather conditions.

The theory of how to 'spiritually' sail or find our way through the mountains and valleys of life is all found in the Bible. The goal of teaching the word of God is to provide us with the knowledge of God's truth and instruction that will equip us to put our faith into practice in the open waters and mountainous terrain of real life. God is the only one who can produce the wind needed to power up our sails, which He does through the powerful wind of the Holy Spirit who energizes us and brings us to life. It goes without saying that unless we harness the wind of the Holy Spirit, we will simply produce a lot of noise and achieve nothing that is of any use to God. As we learn to live in obedience to God's powerful written word, we become disciplined disciples who know how to follow Jesus Christ. Obedience comes through the teaching, preaching and alignment of our lives to the word of God, for without it, it is impossible to be empowered by God. No matter how hard we try, the disciple cannot generate his own power, just as the sailor cannot generate his own wind by attempting to blow onto the sail. The power does not lie in the disciple but entirely in harnessing the wind that God provides.

No Plan

Let's face it. The small church would love to call a well-known, seasoned, experienced pastor, but such a pastor is unlikely to be interested since he is probably only interested in the bigger, well-established church that furthers his career. These days, the small church has no choice but to call a pastor who is new on the scene, or at least, that's how it seems to work. I was already 50 years old and had no idea if I was going to be at WBC for just 5 years or 15 years. Many of the pastors, for whom I have great respect, have been in ministry at the same church for 50 years or more. Over that time, they have lived with the church, providing her with a steady continuity on the journey God has called her to travel. This is similar to the leadership that Moses provided for the Israelites as they wandered through the desert for 40 years. I know that not everyone would agree with that lengthy period, and I have heard some of my own congregation suggest that 6 years is long enough for both the church and the minister. I assume this line of thinking is to allow for a new minister to come along with fresh ideas, a new plan and a new vision. Yet there is always only *one* vision and *one* plan; the vision is Jesus, and the plan is to love God in obedience to the first and greatest commandment, followed by the second, which is to love our neighbour as ourselves.

How can any of us plan how many people God will save over the next five years and aim to hit that target? Can we ever plan God? I was convinced that God did not require a plan to equip His church; He required the church to live in surrender and obedience, together with a clear, unhindered vision of Jesus who leads the way. The aim of my preaching is to help people see these things in the Scriptures and then to go and live it all out.

Choose Life

In the book of Deuteronomy, God presented through Moses a covenant that commanded God's people of Israel to devote themselves to be faithful and Holy unto the Lord their God. If they chose to obey God's commands, He will bless them, but if they chose not to obey, God will curse:

> '*I call heaven and earth to witness against you today, that I have set before you life and death, blessing and curse. Therefore choose life, that you and your offspring may live, loving the LORD your God, obeying his voice and holding fast to him, for he is your life and length of days, that you may dwell in the land that the LORD swore to your fathers, to Abraham, to Isaac, and to Jacob, to give them*' (Deut.30:19–20).

I was convinced that it was God who had called me into *this* church and not another. God had not called me into my own ministry but *His* ministry. He had not called me into my agenda or somebody else's agenda, but *His* agenda. It was clear in my mind that God had called me to call the church to wake up, grow up and love God in obedience to the first and greatest commandment. This was the kind of pastor God was calling me to be.

Chapter 26

FIVE YEARS INTO MINISTRY EVALUATION

I found 2015 to be an extremely challenging year. It marked five years of being a pastor, and I spent the best part of it trying to work out if the church had benefited from my being there. Had my preaching had any effect? Could I clearly see a hunger for the written word of God? Could I see a greater commitment to Christ? Could I see a determined sense of urgency to proclaim the good news of the gospel message to those outside of the church? Could I see the manifest commitment and determination to love the Lord God with life itself? These were the things I was looking for and formed the appraisal of how effective my ministry had been.

Importance of Commitment

By the end of my first five years as a pastor, I had become aware of the particular challenges that come with leading a small church. For any church to function properly, there has to be a firm commitment to Christ first, and out of that to one another. These days, commitment is considered to be a dirty, unattractive, legalistic word. Perhaps this is why in today's free and easy, come and go society, so many couples choose to live together rather than commit themselves to each other in marriage through the bond of love. When somebody signs up to become a member of a local church, they are led to answer confessional questions that relate to their love and commitment to the church:

'Do you commit yourself to love and serve the Lord within the church family, supporting the church, taking a full and active part, seeing your membership as a means to benefit your brothers and sisters in Christ, and to use and develop your gifts to fulfil your ministry for the sake of others and for the glory of God.'

To become a member of a local church but never truly commit to it means that the whole concept of membership is devalued and rendered meaningless.

Disillusionment and Doubt Set In

In year five, the growing number of empty seats on Sunday mornings left me feeling extremely discouraged. I began to question why God had not blessed my ministry, since I had assumed that if He was the one who had called me into ministry, He would surely bless that ministry. My dismay led me to question whether the presence of God was really with me! This reminded me of Moses when he led the Israelites out of Egypt on the way to the Promised Land. Moses petitioned to the Lord:

> *'See, you say to me, "Bring up this people," but you have not let me know whom you will send with me. Yet you have said, "I know you by name, and you have found favour in my sight." Now therefore, if I have found favour in your sight, please show me now your ways, that I may know you in order to find favour in your sight. Consider too that this nation is your people.' And he said to him, 'If your presence will not go with me, do not bring us up from here. For how shall it be known that I have found favour in your sight, I and your people? Is it not in your going with us, so that we are distinct, I and your people from every other people on the face of the earth?'* (Ex. 33:12–16).

I came into ministry knowing all too well that I could do nothing in my own strength or cleverness. I came into ministry *knowing* that I was entirely dependent upon the power and presence of God. I came into ministry *knowing* it was *God's* ministry,

163

not mine. I came into ministry *knowing* that I could not bring about a revival and ongoing spiritual renewal that only God could create and sustain. In my Desert Place, I desired only to possess an authentic faith or none at all, and with that same resolve, I wanted WBC to possess a real, tangible faith that meant everything to them. I wanted nothing false or manufactured but only the real thing. Man produces what is false, and only God can produce the authentic. Only God can make His presence known and transform the lives of people, so why could I not see this happening?

I reasoned many things such as: perhaps I was not the leader the church had expected, wanted or needed. Perhaps she needed someone with more calibre, who had experience in the business world, was entertaining or had a dynamic personality. I had none of those things. In my confusion, I began to question if God really did call me into ministry. Knowing that God never makes mistakes and that He always does what is right, I concluded that I was the one who had failed and got it all wrong. This placed a heavy burden of guilt upon my shoulders: What had I done to my family? I could not understand why God would allow me to uproot my family from our home and friends in Devon all for nothing. Normally, people choose to move from London to Devon, but in a step of faith, trust and obedience, we moved from Devon to London! I was in no way questioning my faith but my calling into ministry.

In addition to this discouragement, the last three months of 2015 were extremely rough. Since October 2015, I had not been feeling right in myself. I had developed a number of unpleasant physical symptoms that included a permanent feeling of peculiarity, as though I were somewhere strange. In addition, I experienced a permanent peculiar taste in my mouth and lost my appetite. A visit to the doctor and blood tests revealed nothing wrong. In the lead up to Christmas, I lost one and a half stone and had frequent moments when I experienced a peculiar smell in my nose that led

to nausea. On New Year's Eve, my left foot began to feel numb
and heavy. At times, my vision took on a glittery effect and I
was becoming very sleepy. I shared nothing with the doctor about
my disillusionment in ministry, but he suggested I might be
suffering from depression and prescribed a prescription for anti-
depressants, which I never redeemed. Nevertheless, my physical
symptoms did seem to coincide with the discouragement of
ministry. I felt as though I was living underneath a heavy thick
dark cloud, which I thought might have more to do with spiritual
oppression rather than depression. This was a confusing time,
which further served to rob me of any assurance I had to my
calling. A Bible verse I found to be extremely challenging, but
one I held on to dearly was:

*'You keep him in perfect peace whose mind is stayed on you
because he trusts in you'* (Isa. 26:3).

As I continued to examine myself and my calling, I became
greatly troubled that I had sinned against God by doubting His
call, and this really disturbed me. Trying as hard as I could to
make sense of what was going on, I knew all too well that the
Devil is always on the prowl, seeking whom he may destroy. I
began to recognize that I had given the Devil a foothold into my
mind, which in turn, sent me to my knees and into a place
of weeping before God in deep repentance. I confessed and
reaffirmed that, *YES*, it *was* God who had called us away from
Devon, and *YES,* it *was* God who had called me to *this* place of
ministry, and *YES*, it *was* a step of faith, trust and obedience, and
YES, I *had* laboured the last five years serving God where He
wanted us to be, and *YES*, I *had* carried out *His* ministry in spite
of the way things looked and felt. With this renewed affirmation,
I began to appreciate that the crucial thing for me to grasp was the
importance of remaining obedient to God and faithful to the
ministry He had called me into. God had called me to be faithful
to the church; He had not called me to be a success as other
people define success, but to shepherd those He had entrusted

into my care. At this very point, the heavy burden of spiritual oppression lifted and has never returned since.

Nonetheless, five years of preaching, teaching and ministry, week in and week out, had not produced the spiritual growth or response I had longed to see and prayed for. I began to question the legitimacy of my moving on to another church.

Chapter 27

DIAGNOSIS OF CANCER

In June 2009, while still at theological college, a nasty looking mole was removed from my back. It was sent off for examination and a subsequent appointment made at the hospital for me to return for the results. On my return, I remember sitting in the consultant's room, waiting to hear what news the consultant had for me. I was told that the mole was a malignant ulcerated melanoma, which is the most aggressive form of skin cancer. It is a high-risk tumour meaning that it has a high risk of spreading (metastasis). The tumour had penetrated to a depth of 1.6mm (stage 2), meaning that they needed to remove more tissue from my back, which they did in July 2009. A few CT scans over the next few months indicated that the cancer had not appeared to spread elsewhere. Even so, they decided to keep a check on me through regular visits to a dermatologist over the next 5 years. In November 2015, I had my final check-up and was given the all-clear.

As the end of 2015 drew near, the physical symptoms that had recently developed continued to persist and I continued to lose weight. My wife asked the doctors if there was a possibility that these symptoms might be related to the malignant melanoma removed from my back in 2009. The GP assured us that this was not the case. However, my wife's sister in Australia, who is a GP, informed us that there was a strong possibility it might be related, and that I should insist on having a brain scan. Eventually my GP relented and booked me in to see a neurologist, who carried out various physical examinations and insisted there was no need for a brain scan. I will never forget her looking me in the eye and telling me that I was fine and there was nothing to worry about. We returned home, but Krissie was not happy with this conclusion and continued to insist that I had a brain scan. On Monday, 29 February 2016, I finally had an MRI scan to my brain. It was my day off and not the best one at that! Krissie was unable to join me, and we both assumed that this was going to be a simple routine procedure. On my way to the hospital, I prayed out loud in the car all the way entrusting myself into God's will and purposes. I prayed the same thing all the way through the scan. As soon as the scan was completed, I expected them to make an appointment for me to come back and see a consultant to get the results. However, the radiographer informed me that they were sending me down to A&E to see a doctor. That did not sound like good news. I spent quite a while waiting in A&E, which left me thinking all kinds of thoughts. After a while, I was called up and told that the scan showed I had intra-cerebral metastases within the brain in the form of five lesions, the largest of which lay within the right temporal lobe and measured 26mm. I was transferred to the Royal Marsden in Chelsea as an inpatient. While there, I had further blood tests which, surprisingly, still showed no abnormalities. I underwent a CT scan and x-rays to establish if the cancer was anywhere else in my body. I approached this scan in the same way as I did the MRI, committing myself wholly to God and praying fervently for Him to establish His purposes. The CT scan revealed the cancer had gone to my body. I had lesions on my liver, spleen, lung and adrenal glands. A liver biopsy confirmed the cancers to be metastasis melanoma stage 4 and connected to the original melanoma I had removed from my back in 2009.

The medical prognosis from the outset was that the cancer was incurable and inoperable. This was terminal. The best the medical profession could do was to give me a new revolutionary chemo treatment called immunotherapy which had shown great promise in its trials. This treatment was stepping into relatively new territory and there was the risk of some very serious side effects, some of which were life-threatening in themselves. This being said, 70% of patients were responding well to the treatment, suffering from no serious side effects so far. If the treatment worked well for me, the most optimistic prognosis suggested that I might still be living a normal life in 10 years' time. For those who did not respond positively, the average life expectancy was around 13 months.

Where Did it Come From?

I can still hear the sound of my dermatologist's voice back in 2009, telling me in her authoritative voice that there is no such thing as a healthy tan. When she first examined the mole on my back, she asked if I had spent any significant time exposed to the Mediterranean sun. The answer, of course, was yes. Even though the malignant mole was dealt with, and I was given the all-clear, the cancer remained hidden away in my body before deciding to give birth to many offspring years later.

Where is God in All of This?

Faith looks to God to make good things happen, not bad things. Nevertheless, faith accepts that bad things might happen but, if the bad does happen, seeks to know where God is in the bad. This diagnosis was thoroughly bad and contained no good. It came as a total shock to both me and Krissie. I had only recently re-affirmed that God had called me to WBC and that this calling was the outworking of His will and purpose. I had been asking in recent times if God wanted me to move on to pastor a different church, so what was I to make of this latest turn of events? During the whole of my time in ministry, I had devoted myself to God in prayer, laying my all before Him and asking Him to have His way in every single part of my life. I now found myself riddled with terminal cancer. Where was God in all of this? I was fully aware that God could have prevented the cancer from taking hold of me, but He did not. Why not?

Perhaps this was God's way of telling me that He was bringing my ministry at WBC to an end? Surely He could do that in some other way that would not have such a devastating impact on my wife and children? From the moment of diagnosis, I tried to figure out how any of this was serving the purposes of God. The situation I found myself in called for me to put into practice everything that God had taught me about faith during the trial of my Desert Place. So many of the lessons I had learnt there were becoming apparent once again.

Treatment Begins

I imagine that most people would have expected me to take sick leave with immediate effect, but I was determined to carry on in ministry while undergoing treatment. In March 2016, the RM Chelsea focused their attention on reducing the severe swelling in my brain by way of a five-day course of whole-brain radiotherapy. This decreased much of the unpleasant physical symptoms I had been experiencing. Needless to say, I lost all the hair on my head and as time passed by it grew back pure white. The radiotherapy was followed up in April 2016 with the first of four 5-day courses of chemo in the form of IV immunotherapy (Ipilimumab and Nivolumab), whose job it was to attack the tumours throughout my brain and body. This dual treatment began with the understanding that if serious side effects occurred, the immunotherapy would need to stop.

Setbacks

Having suffered no serious side effects from the first course of immunotherapy, I received the second course in June, leaving the remaining two to be had in the following months. Unfortunately, in the same week following the second treatment, I began to suffer a physical side effect that affected my right eyelid which had become slightly droopy. Tests were carried out to see why this was happening since they had not experienced this before. As a precautionary measure, the immunotherapy was halted, and I was admitted for tests at the National Hospital for Neurology and Neurosurgery in Queen Square, London. Some of the tests were quite painful, sending electric shocks through wires connected to my hands and face. The results showed that I was suffering from myasthenia gravis, a condition that affects the neuromuscular junction resulting in muscle weakness and fatigability. I was closely examined to see if this condition was going to spread to other parts of my body, such as limbs, swallowing and talking. The doctors concluded that just my eyes had been affected and that I had complex ophthalmoplegia (ocular myasthenia gravis), which is caused by damage to the nerve fibres that coordinate lateral eye movement and control of the eyelids. It was confirmed that this condition had been induced by the immunotherapy treatment I had already received.

Treatment to the eyes began in June 2016 when I became an inpatient at the neurological hospital in Queen Square. I underwent a five-day course of intensive plasma exchange (plasmapheresis), and I could not believe the amount of plasma that was taken out of my body, filling a clear plastic bag the size of a 25kg bag of cement every day. The doctors were fairly confident that this treatment would be successful and expected to see some positive results over the next few days. Unfortunately, there was no change, so I was put on 500mg of IV steroids to see if that would make any difference. This, too, had no effect and the eye condition continued to slowly deteriorate and spread to both eyes. The eye specialist treating me attempted to humour me by telling me that I had been the most unresponsive patient they have ever had! I had no other option but to take that as a compliment.

In August 2016, with no more eye treatment available, the focus shifted back to keeping the cancer under control. Since I could not resume immunotherapy, I was placed on a daily dual tablet form of chemo (Dabrafenib and Trametinib). Apparently, this treatment makes good progress to begin with, stabilizing and even shrinking some of the tumours. However, this treatment has a limited lifespan since, over time, the cancer works out how to adapt and overcome the treatment to gain the upper hand. Additionally, these drugs are extremely powerful and toxic, meaning that nobody knew how long my body would tolerate their presence. The consultants informed me that the average life expectancy for someone starting this treatment was eight months. I began this treatment in August 2016.

At the time of writing this page, it is August 2017. Over the last 12 months or so I have settled into a routine of making trips to the Royal Marsden in Sutton to undergo MRI and CT scans every eight weeks. Alongside these, I have blood tests, observations and consultations every four weeks. While the cancer medication has continued to control the disease and keep me stable, my eyes have continued to slowly deteriorate. I have lost a significant amount of movement in both eyeballs, which means that I need to manoeuvre my head to look at anything. I have virtually lost all the muscle movement in both eyelids and need to tape them up or wear special glasses with props to keep the eyelids open. My vision has doubled, to the extent that in order to focus on something I need to look through my left eye, which is the stronger eye.

Not on the Agenda

As yet, I have not taken any significant sick leave and intend to continue in ministry for as long as I am able. None of us signed up for this when I was first called by the church in 2010. None of us prayed for this or placed it on our 'must do' list. This was new territory for us all.

Since my diagnosis, I have been greatly encouraged by the regular times of prayer for my healing set up by the church. These times of prayer have morphed into praying for the future spiritual health of the church. The leadership team has been very understanding and accommodating, giving me plenty of slack and allowing me to step back while not putting me under any pressure to either step down or step up.

I see my illness as a vital part of my ministry and what God has called me to at this particular point in time. I am determined to take the church with me through this trial, however it ends. I am eager to demonstrate to the church a faith that finds rest in the sufficiency of God's grace and is strong enough to stare death in the face. This is a preparation for the ultimate battle that every Christian must engage with, and the trial of my illness represents real life in all its imperfection and uncertainty. It puts faith to the test, revealing that life is not tidy and there are no neat answers to explain the trials we go through. I have learnt that the important thing is not to know all the answers, but to know Christ. In this way, and with whatever time I have left, I endeavour to lead the church by example.

Chapter 28

WILL GOD HEAL ME?

One of my biggest questions has been to ask God what purpose He has in all of this. I imagine most of us would endure suffering much better if we knew what purpose God had in it all and the good that might come from it. If we had an explanation why God allowed anything to happen, we might be in a better position to make more sense of our trials and gain the much-needed patience to endure them. If only God would let us know why He allows something to happen, rather than keep us in constant suspense as we try to speculate for ourselves. I have done a lot of speculation and examined all the possible reasons why God would call me into ministry at the age of 50, and then after just five years in ministry, allow me to be afflicted with terminal cancer.

I have exhausted myself in prayer, attempting to find new ways to express myself as I ask God for my healing. I have set before Him all my reasons why so much good would flow from my healing and all of the harm and discouragement that my death would create for others. My prayers reflect the fullness of my faith that God is more than capable of totally healing me in an instant, yet I also know that I do not possess the wisdom of God. I do not always see things as He sees things. In all of this, I am left with the uncertainty of not knowing what God will actually do. As I behold the beauty of God's awe-inspiring creation which He simply spoke into being, I am all too aware that God could so easily speak my healing into being.

I have no idea how God does what He does. He is in total control of the whole of human history and is sovereign over everything. My finite mind cannot even begin to comprehend how He works it all together. In the vast splendour of the universe that God created, planet earth does not even register as a minute dot, and on that scale, I do not even exist! Such a thought humbles me because I know that I come under the jurisdiction of such an Almighty, awesome, unfathomable God who has placed me where I am at this particular moment in time. Whether Almighty God heals me or not, I have every good reason to love Him just the same. The Desert Place taught me that God owes me nothing and I owe Him everything. Whatever the outcome of my physical life, I am confident that all is well with my soul and fully satisfied that my salvation is safe in His hands. My hope is not in my healing, and neither is it in this world. My hope is in Christ, who has already given to me the gift of eternal life in the fullness of God's presence and His perfect kingdom.

Does God Always Rescue?

I am sure there are times when God rescues us from something, and we have no idea that He has done so. We have benefited from His protection without ever knowing it. However, I do not have to spend too much time reflecting on the reality of life to know that God does not always rescue His people. We may hear of instances where God has rescued someone from great harm, while at the same time, we know that others have not been rescued from their time of trial.

Does God always rescue us? That question has a double answer for those of us who are in Jesus. On the one hand, the answer is a resounding no, while on the other hand, the answer is a resounding yes.

No, because the evidence of history teaches me that God does not always rescue His people. For example, take into consideration the plight of those 21 Egyptian Coptic Christian 'men of the cross' who were lined up on their knees on the shoreline of the Libyan Sea, paraded in front of the eyes of the world in orange jumpsuits. Their executors stood behind them in menacing black, with knives at the ready. Can you put yourself in any one of those condemned men's shoes and endure their thoughts? I am left wondering if they were praying for God to rescue them. Where was He? They could not see Him; perhaps He was waiting in the wings, ready to step in and intervene at the last moment. Their brutal execution was carried out, which leaves me wondering how God, who sees all things, could remain so passive? Was He paying any attention to their plight? Rescue for those 21 brave men never came, not even a hint of it. As they anticipated their cruel demise, God appeared to be inactive, silent, and nowhere to be seen. By no means were these men the first to suffer like this; neither will they be the last.

How does God hold Himself back from intervening, even for the sake of His own name and reputation? I would like to think that such hideous acts would so infuriate God that He could not possibly withhold Himself from rescuing those in need and administer His swift justice upon the perpetrators. Another example that demonstrates that God does not always come to the rescue of His saints is that of John the Baptist. John found himself languishing in prison for speaking against Herod's unlawful liaisons with his sister-in-law. John and Jesus lived at the same time and in the same geographical neighbourhood. John understood who Jesus really was and what He was capable of doing. If I were in John's shoes, I would hope to think that because I was on the same side as Jesus, it would only be a matter of time before Jesus came along and miraculously rescued me. But no rescue was forthcoming and John, perhaps out of confusion and disillusionment, reminded Jesus of his predicament by sending his own disciples to Jesus. The question he sent them with was: *'Are you the one who is to come, or shall we look for another?'* The reply of Jesus would have left John in no doubt that Jesus was the Messiah. He sent John's disciples back to him with the words, *'Blessed is the one who is not offended by me'* (Luke 7:18–23). Even though Jesus was nearby, there was still no rescue for John, and he met the same fate as those 21 Coptic Christians.

What about the Christians whom the Emperor Nero tied to wooden posts at his garden parties? For the sake of entertainment, he covered them with bitumen, setting them alight as human torches while they were still alive. Yet another Scripture springs to mind. The writer of Hebrews testifies to the persevering faith of those written about in the Old Testament, stating:

'These all died in faith, not having received the things promised, but having seen them and greeted them from afar, and having acknowledged that they were strangers and exiles on the earth' (Heb. 11:13).

'Some were tortured, refusing to accept release, so that they might rise again to a better life. Others suffered mocking and flogging, and even chains and imprisonment. They were stoned, they were sawn in two, they were killed with the sword. They went about in skins of sheep and goats, destitute, afflicted, mistreated of whom the world was not worthy—wandering about in deserts and mountains, and in dens and caves of the earth. And all these, though commended through their faith, did not receive what was promised, since God had planned something better for us so that only together with us would they be made perfect' (Heb. 11:35–40).

There is more. What about the stoning of Stephen in Acts 7? Suffering the agony of being beaten to death with stones is not a nice way to die. Surely the newly born infant church desperately needed someone like Stephen? Surely God needed Stephen to help spread the good news about the salvation found only in Jesus? Even so, no rescue came for Stephen. These few examples all reflect the reality of living out a real faith in a real world that is Christless and full of darkness. It is a faith where there is no rescue but, rather, execution. It is a faith that does not depend upon rescue but accepts persecution and execution as something that accompanies and demonstrates a real living faith. Such faith bears witness to a hope that is not in this world. Nevertheless, the

Bible does record occasions where some have been dramatically rescued. In Acts 12, we read that Peter had been put in prison, facing certain execution. Herod had recently put James to death by the sword and most likely had similar plans for Peter. On this occasion, God chose to rescue Peter even though He did not choose to rescue James. On another occasion, we read in Acts 16 how God rescued Paul and Silas from prison. On both these occasions, God chose to rescue Peter and Paul, but there came a time later on when He chose not to rescue either of them and both were executed because of their faith.

The point is, God *can* rescue any saint from persecution anytime He so chooses. More often than not, it appears that He doesn't but chooses to allow His saints to be put to death. Even so, the Bible tells us that a future Day of Judgment and justice will eventually come, a Day in which God will no longer remain hidden or silent. On that Day, He will step in and intervene to call to account every act that has rebelled against Him. On that Day, God will administer His Holy justice and see that His saints receive their redemption, retribution, vindication and reward for remaining faithful.

So, while God *can* and *could* rescue His people from death by persecution, the evidence points to the fact that most of the time He chooses not to. The question I now ask is: can the same be said about God rescuing His saints who suffer cruel and deadly physical afflictions by healing them? I have no hesitation in answering yes. God *can* and *could* rescue His people, but most of the time chooses not to. Some might disagree with this comparison, claiming that death by persecution is in a completely different league to death by disease or sickness. Death by persecution brings glory and honour to God through the one who demonstrates by *choice* that they are prepared to pick up their cross and die for their faith in Jesus. On the other hand, death by disease or sickness is not a choice, for no one *chooses* to die in such a way. If anything, disease and sickness results in premature death and is a sign of weakness and defeat that in no way bears testimony to the power of God's kingdom; rather, it reflects the domain of darkness and evil. But to what degree is this true? While disease and sickness most definitely do not characterize the kingdom of God, neither does being put to death by persecution. Death, however it comes, never represents God's kingdom but always demonstrates the fallen world we live in. The god and ruler of this present world is the Devil, and we are surrounded by the presence of sin and darkness with all of its hideous consequences. Whether death comes through persecution or sickness, the Christian's witness is to be the same. In and through both, we press on to take the kingdom by force, faithfully bearing witness to the sufficiency of God's grace and the salvation we have in Jesus. We press on, in the sure knowledge that it's not our earthly body that counts but our soul, understanding that this fallen body is temporal, but our soul is eternal. We press on in the sure hope that God will give to those who overcome in Christ a new glorified body at His return and '*the crown of life, which God has promised to those who love him*' (James 1:12). Whether in persecution or sickness, both present us with a powerful witness to Jesus and His salvation power.

Sometimes, people have tried to encourage me by telling me a story they heard of someone who God healed of cancer. Nevertheless, while I am very happy for such people, I do not find these stories helpful in the way I am sure they are intended. The thing is, it is not as though I do not already believe that God has the power and authority to heal me. I am one hundred per cent convinced that the Creator and sustainer of the universe is more than capable of performing what is for Him, such a simple thing. What I do not know is whether He *will* heal me. Just because God heals someone does not mean that He is obliged to heal me or everyone else. While only a few of us may know of first-hand instances where God has rescued someone from terminal illness, the vast majority of us know of many more Christians who God has not healed and who have died from their sickness. Are we to assume that those who received healing were healed because they had the required level of faith to be healed?

Are we to assume that the vast majority who were not healed did not have enough faith to be healed? I dare to say no. Just two examples I know of are enough to convince me of this. In the 1980s, there were two well-known Christian evangelical leaders in their forties. Both men enjoyed thriving ministries and international influence. Both men were in their prime and both headed up large, lively churches which were very much influenced by charismatic theology. Both fully believed in the spiritual gift of healing as well as all the other charismatic gifts. The time came when both men were inflicted with cancer. Both their churches prayed fervently for healing and believed for their healing, but the healing never came and both men died from their cancer. Why was this so? Since these men were men of faith, I do not believe for one moment that their deaths were the result of a lack of faith. I dare say that various explanations have been suggested why their faith did not work the miracle they had prayed for and had expected. We can speculate as much as we like, but at the end of the day, we have to be content not to know why they did not receive healing. What this teaches me is that while God can and could rescue any of His saints from terminal disease, we cannot insist that He does so.

The reality of life teaches us that babies and young children die. They have died so young that they have been denied the opportunity of growing old enough to gain the knowledge and understanding of the difference between right and wrong, good and evil. Knowing the difference between good and evil, right and wrong, robbed Adam and Eve of the utopia they once enjoyed in the Garden of Eden. As a result of their rebellion against God, they were cursed by Him for their disobedience, a curse that led to the death of their state of perfection and innocence, and their eyes opened to know the difference between right and wrong, good and evil. Although I cannot be adamant about this, my understanding from what I read in the Bible suggests that babies and young children who do not know the difference between good or bad, right or wrong, remain in a state of innocence and therefore stand in the saving grace of God which ushers them into heaven when they die. Nevertheless, their early deaths present us all with the awareness of how ugly and destructive death is, especially when it comes to those who are so helpless and naive. Most of us protest at why God allows infants and babies to die so young in the first place; surely, they deserved to live a longer life? Nevertheless, what if the early death of an infant might turn out to be a blessing, shielding them from experiencing the pain and torment that life in a fallen world often brings? If this is true, what compensation!

The reality of life proves that many faithful Christians die well before reaching old age. They are robbed of life early through an assortment of various diseases, fatal accidents, crime and natural disasters. Their deaths seem so unfair because they, too, died in a state of innocence that played no part in whatever led to their deaths.

Consider the attack on the Twin Towers in 2011. That destructive event killed thousands of people, regardless of who they were, how old they were or how good they were. Similarly, when a tower in Siloam fell on 18 people and killed them, some people were looking to Jesus to provide them with an explanation. The comment Jesus made was this:

'Do you think they were worse offenders than all the others who lived in Jerusalem? No, I tell you; but unless you repent, you will all likewise perish' (Luke 13:4–5).

Jesus did not explain *why* those 18 people died at that given moment and in that way. However, His reply highlights that we are all sinners who will die one way or another, and that before that happens, we all need to repent of our sin. The point Jesus makes is not that we will escape physical death if we repent, but that if we do not repent *before* we die, we will perish *after* we have died. Jesus's comment relates to the Judgment Day that all sinners will have to face after the physical death of their bodies. All who have not repented but have died in their sin will perish in that dreadful place where they are banished from God's goodness and presence for the whole of eternity. On the other hand, John 3:16 teaches us that whoever believes in Jesus will *not* perish after death, but will go on to enjoy eternal life in all of the fullness of God's glorious goodness and presence; what a contrast! This suggests that the worst thing that can happen to any of us is not death itself, but to die in our sin. If we die in our sin, then we will perish in what the Bible calls hell. None of us can be sure when our time will come or how it will come. What we have to be sure of is our readiness for the unexpected. The most important question is not whether God always rescues us from an early, unpleasant death, but rather, are we right with God when the moment of death does arrive?

Does God always rescue those who belong to Him? No, not in this life, but yes, God always rescues us *from* this life *for* the next. For those who belong to Christ in this life, no matter how short or long that life may be, the best is yet to come but not in this world as we know it. For this reason, whatever outcome awaits me in this life, I know that in the end, cancer does not win; Jesus does. While He may not rescue me in this life, He will rescue me, not *from* death but *through* death.

Looking at the bigger picture, God has *already* rescued me. Cancer may very well condemn and destroy my earthly body, but my spirit has already been completely healed of the most hideous, destructive disease that anyone could ever be inflicted with: the spiritual disease of sin. Through faith in Christ, my spirit has already been rescued and delivered from the power of sin and death. As I face death in the physical body, I rejoice as I await a glorious, future inheritance in God's perfect kingdom. I look forward with great anticipation to the future redemption of my body when Christ returns. The Apostle Paul wrote: *'But as it is written, "What no eye has seen, nor ear heard, nor the heart of man imagined, what God has prepared for those who love him"'* (1 Cor. 2:9). I can live this life in the knowledge and hope of the blessing my salvation gives to me each new day. God blesses me every day with so much more than I ever need, but the greatest blessing is to know Jesus as my Saviour and Lord of my life. Death cannot destroy this eternal blessing, but rather serve me well by releasing me into the eternal blessing of my Saviour's presence.

But What About...?

The Bible records the miraculous power that Jesus demonstrated while He lived on earth, proving Himself to be the Son of God. He demonstrated His authority over the realm of nature; for example, He calmed a vicious storm while in a boat with His terrified disciples on the Lake of Galilee (Mark 4). He turned five loaves and two fishes into a feast that fed over five thousand people (Mark 6). He instantly healed everyone who came to Him for healing. He made the lame walk, the blind see and the deaf to hear. On three separate occasions, Jesus raised people from the dead who had recently died (John 11 – Mark 5 – Luke 7). In Matthew 4:24, we read:

'So his fame spread throughout all Syria, and they brought him all the sick, those afflicted with various diseases and pains, those oppressed by demons, those having seizures, and paralytics, and he healed them.'

These supernatural miracles were signs that pointed to who Jesus really was and where He had come from. Because of these signs, people paid attention to the importance of the message He preached concerning the good news about the kingdom of heaven.

Jesus told His followers: *'ALL authority in heaven and on earth has been given to me'* (Matt. 28:18).

I am a follower of Jesus and wholeheartedly believe that Jesus still has the authority to do extraordinary things today. Even though I have exhausted myself by asking Him to heal me, He has not. As I have asked, I have had the following words of Jesus pulsating through my mind:

'And I tell you "Ask, and it will be given to you; seek, and you will find; knock, and it will be opened to you. For everyone who asks receives; the one who seeks finds; and to the one who knocks, the door will be opened"' (Luke 11:9).

'And Jesus answered them, "Truly, I say to you, if you have faith and do not doubt, you will not only do what has been done to the fig tree, but even if you say to this mountain, 'Be taken up and thrown into the sea,' it will happen. And whatever you ask in prayer, you will receive, if you have faith."' (Matt. 21:21–22).

'Truly, I say to you, whatever you bind on earth shall be bound in heaven, and whatever you loose on earth shall be loosed in heaven. Again I say to you, if two of you agree on earth about anything they ask, it will be done for them by my Father in heaven' (Matt. 18:18–19).

'And this is the confidence that we have toward him, that if we ask anything according to his will he hears us. And if we know that he hears us in whatever we ask, we know that we have the requests that we have asked of him' (1 John 5:14).

'If you abide in me, and my words abide in you, ask whatever you wish, and it will be done for you. By this my Father is glorified, that you may bear much fruit and so prove to be my disciples' (John 15:7).

'Whatever you ask in my name, this I will do, that the Father may be glorified in the Son. If you ask me anything in my name, I will do it' (John 14:13–14).

The above Scriptures have the potential to send me into an overwhelming mood of discouragement, rather than the joy of wonderful encouragement. They appear to be promises, but they have proved to be anything but. You may tell me till you are blue in the face that these Scriptures always work if they are combined with faith, but my experience, which is firmly embedded in the reality of a real faith in a real life, tells me that they do not because they have not. Therefore, what these promises speak to me is that prayer does not work in the way we would like it to.

I have done and prayed all of the above. While I have grown weary in prayer, I have never given up asking in Jesus's name for my healing. I do not use the name Jesus as though that is some kind of magic word to ensure that I get what I want; rather, I pray as someone who *lives in* Jesus, and so I pray from *within* my relationship to Him. Whenever I come to God in prayer, my approach is like that of the leper who knelt before Jesus, imploring Him:

> "*If you will, you can make me clean.*" *Moved with pity, he stretched out his hand and touched him and said to him, "I will; be clean*" (Mark 1:40–41).

Taking all of the above Scriptures at face value, they tell me that if I have faith, Jesus will most assuredly grant my request to heal me. These Scriptures appear to promise that I will have my healing if I ask in faith. I have asked, begged, pleaded for Jesus to heal me, knowing that for the Creator of the universe this is no hard thing. Yet still I have not received my healing.

Chapter 29

WHY DOES GOD REFUSE TO HEAL ME?

It is obvious that I cannot ask God to do anything that is inconsistent with His character. I cannot ask for anything that is evil, unjust or those things that promote my own selfish ambition. I cannot ask God for such things and expect Him to listen to me, let alone answer such requests. But why does God refuse to answer a request that only promotes what is good and beneficial, such as my healing? I am faced with several options to choose from:

God Does Not Exist

Let me say from the outset, I am completely convinced that God does exist! I am someone who has tremendous admiration for the great outdoors. I marvel at the natural world with all of its diversity, colour, smells and sounds. I marvel at the ocean and everything found in it. I marvel at the skies and everything that flies through them. I marvel at the different continents with their mountains, valleys, plants, flowers, forests and the animal kingdom. I stand amazed as I look up at the sky and see the sun, moon and stars sitting in the vast expanse of an endless universe with all of its galaxies. I look at the design of my body and the gift of life which enables my body to function. With my mind, I stand in wonder and awe as I behold all of these things. Even the atheist, who denies the existence of a Creator God, is impressed and amazed by what they see. I do so even more since I recognize the God who is the source of all of its beauty, order, and majesty, all of which reflect the glory of the one who created it. If creation is so awesome, inspiring and uplifting, how much more the one who designed and put it all together?

I fail to comprehend how anyone can marvel at creation and its design yet believe that it all came together out of nothing and by a random chance of sequential events. The overwhelming evidence for a God who designed it all is plain for all to see; it sits there on display right in front of our eyes. I do not need the Bible to tell me there is a God since the evidence for His existence is so obvious! The atheist will argue that if God exists, why do we not see Him? Why, after all these years of human history, does God remain hidden? His absence, they say, simply proves the fact that He does not exist; If God does exist and He is all good and powerful, why does He allow so much suffering in the world to take place? What is stopping Him from getting rid of all the evil and bad things so that we can all live in peace, harmony and happiness? These are logical questions that deserve to be answered, which is what the Bible does. The Bible tells me that God's original creation contained no evil or bad things and that the earth was full of peace, harmony and happiness. The Bible also tells me why God remains hidden from our sight. It also tells me that about two thousand years ago, God did show up to become one of us, revealing Himself to humanity in the human form of Jesus. God sent His Son from heaven into the world to reveal that He does exist and who He is.

This leads me to the second reason that I believe that God exists. Some might say that, outside of the Bible, there is no proof that the historical Jesus ever existed. However, one only has to look into the writings of some of the great historians of Jesus's day to see that He was indeed a historical person. The Bible reveals to me the historical Jesus, that He was born, lived, was crucified and raised from the dead three days later. Forty days after His resurrection, Jesus ascended back into heaven from where He came. Jesus Christ said He had come *from* God and was sent *by* God. In Jesus, God became a man of flesh and blood. Science is incapable of explaining God or proving that He does not exist. Neither can science explain who Jesus was since He was 100% human and 100% God.

'For in him the whole fullness of deity dwells bodily' (Col. 2:9).

'He was in the world, and the world was made through him, yet the world did not know him. He came to his own, and his own people did not receive him' (John 1:10–11).

Through what He taught and what He did, Jesus revealed that there is only *one* God and who that God is. He has also shown us the only way to be reconciled to God,

'Jesus said to him, "I am the way, and the truth, and the life. No one comes to the Father except through me"' (John 14:6).

I am Not a Christian

Perhaps God does not heal me because I am not a genuine Christian. Perhaps I am deluded, living under the illusion that I am a Christian, but in reality, my faith is false. How can this be? Many people claim to be a Christian but do not live a life that demonstrates a real faith that reveals a commitment to Christ and His interests. Perhaps they consider themselves to be Christian because they were born into a so-called Christian country, or perhaps they go to church once in a while.

How do I *know* that I am a genuine Christian? What defines me as a Christian is that not only do I believe in the God and Father of Jesus Christ, but I also recognize that I am a sinner who has sinned against this same God. Such recognition, brought to light by the conviction of the Holy Spirit, has led me into a profound awareness of my sin, compelling me to repent and turn away from my sin whilst turning towards God. Turning to God means putting all of my faith and trust in Christ, whom God sent to be my Saviour and who saves me from my sin. Jesus tells me that whoever believes in Him will not perish but have everlasting life (John 3:16). If I do not consider myself to be a Christian, I am making Jesus out to be a liar and a fraud. However, I take Jesus Christ at His word and, since I do believe and place my faith in Him, I am qualified by Christ to be a Christian.

There is yet more evidence that I am a Christian. When somebody possesses a true, authentic faith in Christ Jesus and turns to God, Jesus places God the Holy Spirit into that person as a sign from heaven that they really do belong to Him. I do not physically see the Holy Spirit residing in me, just as I cannot see my own spirit dwelling in me. Whilst this is so, I can experience the effects and evidence of the Holy Spirit's indwelling, who has brought my spirit to life which initiates a desire that *wants* to live in communion with God and obedience to Him. That same desire looks forward to the day when my life on earth will be drawn to an end, and I am ushered into the presence of God where my desire will become fully made manifest. This desire is not something I have created myself; it has been put there by God through my faith in Jesus. This is not a feeling; it is the effect of the Holy Spirit confirming my spiritual union with Christ.

God Does Not Really Care

Perhaps God will not heal me because He does not really care? The Bible teaches me that God is all-powerful, does no wrong and makes no mistakes: all of His ways are just and perfect, and nothing is impossible for Him. If that is the case, why is it right and perfect for Him not to answer my prayers for my healing? At times, it would be very easy to feel as though God does not really like me very much; if He did, why would He inflict me with cancer in the first place? God has allowed me to be smitten, not with just one isolated lesion but multiple lesions scattered throughout the organs of my body and brain. God seems to have done a thorough job of making sure that I have plenty of cancers that are designed to kill me. If this is not enough, God has allowed me to be afflicted with the very frustrating side effect to both my eyes caused by the original cancer treatment. All of these afflictions make it far more challenging and quite draining as I prepare, preach and seek to fulfil my responsibilities as a pastor. What is more, God has not permitted any of the treatment to my eyes to succeed, but rather to grow steadily worse. If I am still not convinced that, perhaps, God does not care, I must surely be persuaded by the fact that God does not seem to pay any attention to the many prayers for healing offered up by others and myself. In accordance with James 5:14, I have been anointed with oil several times yet without effect. How am I to believe that God cares for me, my wife and family, when all the evidence above points in the opposite direction! Does God *really* care? If He does, He has a strange way of showing it!

In my natural self, the man of flesh who belongs to and thinks like this world, it would be easy to persuade myself that the overwhelming evidence concludes that God doesn't really care. I arrive at this conclusion as I converse with my feelings which can be extremely persuasive. Yet there is something that speaks with a far more powerful voice which convinces me that God *does* care. I see the supreme reality of this care in the overwhelming evidence of the cross that clearly demonstrates the supremacy of God's love towards me.

While the act of God's love took place at the cross on just one given day in history, its powerful effect is limitless and endless. The fact that God the Father sent God the Son from heaven to earth to demonstrate His love tells me that God *does* care. The fact that Jesus came, not to condemn me but to save me from the condemnation of my own sin, tells me that God *does* care. Jesus came to seek and save the lost, and that includes me. He came to meet my most desperate need, a need I could never meet myself. God *chose* to bring me, a sinner, to Himself and has predestined me to be conformed into the likeness of His own precious Son. Furthermore, through the cross of Christ and His resurrection, God has granted to me an eternal heavenly inheritance. Faced with such compelling evidence, I am not permitted to even entertain the idea that God does not care for me, nor allow the natural man, who is driven by feelings, dictate to my faith what is a blatant lie.

There will never be a shortage of people who accuse God of not caring, especially when disaster and tragedy strike good and innocent people. Does God really care? Yes, and the evidence, which does not satisfy everyone, is seen through the supremacy of the cross of Christ. There is a passage in the Bible that brings me great comfort:

> *'So we do not lose heart. Though our outer self is wasting away, our inner self is being renewed day by day. For this light and momentary affliction is preparing for us an eternal weight of glory beyond all comparison, as we look not to the things that are seen but to the things that are unseen. For the things that are seen are transient, but the things that are unseen are eternal'* (2 Cor. 4:16–18).

The accusation that God does not care leads us into a pitiful state of feeling hard done by, cheated, picked on and treated unfairly. Consider Jesus; He lived a sinless life of perfect obedience to God the Father. Within the whole of human history, Jesus was the only person who did not deserve to die or suffer in any way. Yet God not only allowed Jesus to suffer, He *ordained* His suffering. Does this provide us with the evidence that God did not care for or love His own Son? At the pinnacle of His suffering, Jesus cried out in a loud voice, *'My God, my God, why have you forsaken me?'* (Matt. 27:46). It is at this point that Jesus, the Son of man who took upon Himself the penalty of our sin, experienced God's total abandonment and rejection. If anyone had good reason to accuse God of not caring or being unfair, it was Jesus. Yet Jesus, the Son of God, saw the bigger picture of what was really going on as He looked ahead to His resurrection that lay beyond the other side of the cross.

God is Not in Control

Having established that God *does* care about me, perhaps He is unable to heal me simply because He is not in control. If God is not in control of my affairs in this life, then my faith only really counts once this life comes to its natural end. When the final battle of death is completed, that is the point where God takes over control and leads me into His presence, where my salvation is fully realized. In the meantime, perhaps the only effect faith has upon my life in the present time is to comfort me with that future hope. In this case, the best I can hope for in life is to hope for good fortune and luck, taking whatever life dishes out as best I can, striving to survive and enjoy life for as long as I possibly can.

Throughout the last 23 years of my life, I have tried to see where the hand of God has been at work. In the last two years, this has somewhat intensified for obvious reasons. I look at all the prayers offered up to God that have asked for my healing, yet they continue to go unanswered. This calls into question the point of prayer. What is the point in praying if our prayers go unanswered? Perhaps God cannot answer them because He is not in control and has no other option but to let nature take its natural course and allow Satan to take the upper hand.

We live in a fallen world and have no choice but to expect that bad things will happen. If God is not in control, then God's presence is restricted to being that of an observer, watching from the sidelines and powerless to step in and intervene. When trouble hits, God has no choice but to leave us to our own devices to fight our battles without Him. If this is the case and God is powerless to respond to our prayers, why bother to pray for healing or anything else? If God is not in control, then prayer can never work and serves no meaningful purpose. Our prayers simply reflect the spiritualization of our wishful thinking. Perhaps those small prayers we have prayed, and that God seemed to answer, would have happened anyway by chance!

However, the Bible *encourages* us to pray and to pray without ceasing (1 Thess. 5:17). Why would the Apostle Paul teach this if God were not in control?

The Bible teaches me about the character and nature of God. God is the Creator and ruler of the universe. He is the source of all moral and spiritual authority: the Supreme Being. He is all-knowing and nothing ever takes Him by surprise. Nothing can happen unless it accords with His will because in all things God is sovereign. Therefore, I have to believe that God is *always* in control; if He is not in control, then how can He be God? If my life does not come under God's complete control, then my life as a follower of Christ is destined to be full of fear, anxiety and worry. What is more, if God does not have ultimate control over my cancer, how can I be sure that He has control over my salvation?

As I continue to pray for my healing, I cannot pray for something that I do not believe God is capable of doing. Additionally, I cannot pray for something expecting God to do what I ask as though He is my personal genie. Am I to treat God as though He *must* demonstrate His ability to control by insisting that He carry out my wishes? No. If that is my wish, then all I am doing is insisting that I am the one who is in control and God is at my beck and call. Convinced that God has both the power and authority to exercise His control, I continue to ask Him for my healing. It is not up to me whether He grants my desire or not, but either way, I have the faith to believe that God is ultimately always in control, no matter how things feel, look or turn out.

I Embrace Unconfessed Sin

Perhaps the only reason God withholds His healing from me is due to some kind of unconfessed sin in my life. This could be something from my past that I have not dealt with or something in the present that I am holding on to and refuse to let go. This possibility is a valid point, and so I have deeply examined myself to see if there is any unconfessed sin that prevents me from receiving the blessing of God's healing. In humility, I can honestly say that my conscience is clear. I constantly live in repentance, knowing that repentance and confession is to be a way of life and the mark of holiness. In this I continue to be thankful for God's ongoing grace and mercy.

The reality is, no matter how hard I might try, I am incapable of living in constant obedience to the first and greatest commandment. Jesus told an enquirer what the greatest commandment is:

> *'You shall love the Lord your God with all your heart and with all your soul and with all your mind. This is the first and greatest commandment. And a second is like it: You shall love your neighbor as yourself'* (Matt. 22:37–39).

If I lived in perfect obedience to the above commands, then I would live as a perfect man. The reality is I am not a perfect man since I was born into imperfection; I am an imperfect man living in an imperfect world, which does not make for a good recipe! With no deliberate intention or desire and because of my fallen nature, I still have the ability to disobey and sin every single day. Every time I do, say or think something that does not express love for God, friend or enemy, I sin against God. These constant failings and weaknesses go to show how imperfect I am and how dependent I am upon the perfection and righteousness of Christ.

The following Scripture teaches me that I still sin, even though I stand in the rightness of Christ. That sin must be recognized and confessed:

> *'Is anyone among you sick? Let him call for the elders of the church, and let them pray over him, anointing him with oil in the name of the Lord. And the prayer of faith will save the one who is sick, and the Lord will raise him up. And if he has committed sins, he will be forgiven. Therefore, confess your sins to one another and pray for one another, that you may be healed'* (James 5:14–16).

I live daily in the confidence of knowing that in Christ I am forgiven of all my sin. I know that my conscience is clear before God and that I do not embrace any sin that is holding back my healing.

I Have Not Tried the Right Prayer Methods

Perhaps God is unable to heal me because I am not using the correct prayer methods that will *unlock* my healing. The TV evangelist confidently tells me with a voice of absolute authority that there is power in my words, and it is up to me to command my cancer to leave. I wholeheartedly agree that our words are very powerful. What we say has the power to create a negative or positive environment. Our words have the power to either build up and encourage others or the power to pull them down and destroy. Our words have the power to speak the truth and enlighten, or to tell lies and deceive. Our words carry authority, which we use to our advantage in our capacity as parents, teachers and leaders. Perhaps I will obtain my healing by using my words of authority to command my cancer to leave me, naming and claiming it by confessing my healing as though it has already taken place. However, I do not find any of the above suggestions helpful. We must be very careful not to take Scriptures out of their proper context, for if we do, we can get the Bible to say just about anything we want it to say.

With all these suggestions, I have to question whether people resort to these well-intentioned methods because they have come to the conclusion that ordinary prayer has simply not worked for them. More questions follow; if ordinary prayer does not work, then what is ordinary prayer all about? Some people have suggested I visit a Christian Healing Centre, to which I ask why? Do I really have to go to a certain place to receive healing? While I dare say there is a lot of comfort and support to be had in attending these places, I have to ask what this says about the value of the many prayers offered up to God by the church. Are the prayers of the church ineffective because those prayers are not good enough or sufficiently anointed? Is the Holy Spirit, who dwells in me, not sufficiently anointed to respond to my simple request that asks for God to heal me? Is the name of Jesus, in whom I ask, not a sufficient authority? One thing I know; Jesus is all-sufficient, and I am satisfied with the simplicity of presenting my requests to Him. The rest is up to Him.

I Lack the Faith to be Healed

Some might say that God cannot heal me because I lack the faith to be healed. They say I do not have enough faith or the right kind of faith and must step out and exercise boldness of faith. But this verdict does not provide me with a satisfactory explanation. My faith in Christ tells me that He can do the impossible, calm any storm, heal any sickness and raise the dead. It would be such an easy thing for Jesus to heal me completely and instantly. Since Jesus is the One who sustains the whole of creation by His powerful word and will one day raise everyone from the dead, I have no difficulty believing in His power and authority to heal me. If I am to believe that I do not have enough faith to be healed, I am left feeling discouraged and disillusioned. This is because the ongoing absence of my healing demonstrates that I have proved to be incapable of creating enough faith to be healed. The implication is that I will not obtain my healing until I make more effort and get enough faith. How am I to resolve this crippling deficiency? This is confusing. If my healing is dependent upon my own ability to self-create faith, then my faith in Jesus and dependency upon Him to heal me is made redundant. In effect, I have to heal myself!

Those who hold to a strong 'Kingdom Now' theology might suggest that my healing will be unlocked once I fully realize who I am in Christ. As a royal son of the King, I must claim my divine rights and privileges that come with my status as a citizen of God's kingdom. I am a royal son of the King, and all I need to do is claim my right to be healed and receive it as though it is already mine. My failure to do this not only demonstrates my lack of

196

faith, but also a failure to grasp and understand my true identity in Christ. Therefore, I cannot receive healing because I am not living in the victorious blessings of the kingdom life to be enjoyed in this life... or so it goes.

The 'lack of faith' line of reasoning carries with it an extremely damaging side effect that questions my very salvation. If I do not receive my healing because I am unable to create enough faith, how can I ever be sure that I am able to generate enough faith in Jesus to receive from Him salvation from my sins? Is having the faith in Jesus to be physically healed a different kind of faith to the one that believes that Jesus can heal me of the spiritual disease of sin and be saved? How can I be sure that the faith I have in Jesus to save me is adequate and effective? Am I to name and claim my salvation? Am I to use the power of my words to command my salvation to become a reality? Has it ever been the case that my ability to be healed of the most terrible, spiritual disease anyone can ever have, depended upon how much faith I can generate myself? Or is my faith, whether for healing or salvation, a gift of God's grace and mercy? Let me ask a few questions: What requires the greatest faith; to be healed of cancer or to be healed of sin and receive salvation? Which is the greatest and most powerful miracle; to be healed of cancer or to be healed of sin and receive salvation?

My point is this. If I lack the faith for Jesus to heal me of cancer and my eye defect, then I most certainly lack the faith for Jesus to heal me of sin. The latter is supremely greater than the former. If I am incapable of generating enough faith to be physically healed, then I am damned and condemned since I stand no chance of creating enough faith that Jesus will heal me of my sin. Such an approach robs me of the assurance, joy and trust that I have in Christ, adding to my existing burden of suffering from cancer.

'And behold, some people brought to him a paralytic, lying on a bed. And when Jesus saw their faith, He said to the paralytic, "Take heart, my son; your sins are forgiven."

197

And behold, some of the scribes said to themselves, "This man is blaspheming." But Jesus, knowing their thoughts, said, "Why do you think evil in your hearts? For which is easier, to say, 'Your sins are forgiven,' or to say, 'Rise and walk'? But that you may know that the Son of Man has authority on earth to forgive sins"—He then said to the paralytic— "Rise, pick up your bed and go home." And he rose and went home' (Matt. 9:2–7).

God Does Not Want Me to be Healed

I dare say that those of the charismatic persuasion think I have lost the plot even to ask such a crazy question. They would say, 'Of course God wants you to be healed: He is that kind of a God!' It would be very easy to go along with that line of reasoning, but with all the evidence that points to my lack of healing, I have to look much deeper into this question.

Consider 1 Timothy 2:4, which tells me that God *'desires all people to be saved and come to the knowledge of truth.'* Does this mean that if God *desires* something to happen, it *must* take place? If this is so, how are we to understand the many Scriptures that teach that not all people will be saved from the eternity of hell?

So, I have to ask, does God desire my healing? If He does, why does He refuse to respond to all of my prayers for healing? Since God has not healed me, does this suggest that God does not desire for me to be healed? This has been one of the biggest questions that I struggle to answer. I know that God is sovereign, an attribute of God which I do not claim to fully comprehend or understand. What I do know is that God always does what is right.

I have no difficulty in believing that God can heal me, but I do not know if He is going to 'will' it to happen. If God does not want to heal me, He must surely have a greater purpose for not doing so.

I find it difficult to work out the meaning of all this since God has not told me what that greater purpose is. Where is the good that comes through my illness and death? Perhaps God wants me to wait until I get to heaven to see the reality of this goodness, but if this is so, at what point and in what way does it work out for the good of my wife? This I do not know, and I have no easy answers. What I do know is that I need to have the faith to be content with the sovereignty of God.

God is Punishing Me and Wants Me to Suffer

The above sub-heading forces me to make a clear distinction between those who belong to Christ and those who do not. Those who do not are under the curse of God and will suffer from His eternal punishment in hell, whereas those who belong to Christ come under the eternal blessing of God and are rewarded in His eternal kingdom.

The truth is, I know that my own sin condemns me. I know that I cannot stand before a Holy God and escape His justice and punishment. That being said, I also know that I will escape that punishment because Jesus took all of my punishment upon Himself at the cross. In this I am confident, since I have recognized my sinful condition, turned away from my sinful life and placed my faith in Jesus to save me from my sin. Since I belong to Jesus, I do not fear the condemnation of my sin or the judgment of God (Rom. 8:1). Jesus has set me free from those things. As a son of God, I live in the peace that God does not punish His children. What He does do, however, is discipline His children. The writer of Hebrews writes:

> *'It is for discipline that you have to endure. God is treating you as sons. For what son is there whom his father does not discipline? If you are left without discipline, in which all have participated, then you are illegitimate children and not sons. Besides this, we have had earthly fathers who disciplined us and we respected them. Shall we not much*

more be subject to the Father of spirits and live? For they disciplined us for a short time as it seemed best to them, but he disciplines us for our good, that we may share his holiness. For the moment all discipline seems painful rather than pleasant, but later it yields the peaceful fruit of righteousness to those who have been trained by it' (Heb. 12: 7–11).

This passage tells me that if I really am a child of God, I must expect my faith to be tested by hardships and that God uses these to discipline me for my good. God uses my trials to train me, with the end result leading to righteousness and peace. Therefore, I recognize that God may well be using my cancer, not to punish me, but to discipline me. There is a big difference between the two. This raises another question. If God is sovereign and always in control, then I have to conclude that God is the one who must take ultimate responsibility for my affliction. Am I accusing God of punishing me? No. I am simply acknowledging the sovereignty of God to do what He pleases. Whether He is using the agency of Satan I do not know. What I do know is that God is using my affliction for my good and His purposes. Do I understand this? No, not at this present moment in time, but I am certain that the 'good' will become apparent at some point in the future.

Suffering

Punishment leads to a form of suffering. A convicted criminal is sent to prison to suffer the punishment of his crime by isolation from the rest of society and for the protection of society. He is denied his freedom as a means to pay for his crime. Some people dislike the word punishment, preferring to use the word rehabilitation. However, the punishment of eternal damnation is not going to act as some kind of rehabilitation process that cleans up sinners and give them a second chance. Once in hell, always in hell! We have just seen that when a follower of Christ suffers, they are not being punished by God but possibly disciplined. That discipline may very well serve as some kind of rehabilitation to get a Christian back onto the right track. The work Jesus completed at the cross was a one-off act of complete restoration on our behalf, resulting in our salvation. Thus, the repentant sinner is set free from the punishment of their sin, no longer living under the sentence of God's judgment, but under His grace and blessing. From here on, the Holy Spirit continues His work of transformation, turning the sinner into a saint while placing within them a hatred of sin and a love for God. This is an ongoing work that takes place for the rest of the saint's earthly life and will sometimes necessitate that God allows us to suffer in order to humble us, correct us, prepare us and grow us into a greater dependency upon Him. Jesus told the saints in the church at Smyrna to be prepared to suffer persecution:

'Do not fear what you are about to suffer. Behold the devil is about to throw some of you into prison that you may be tested and for ten days you will have tribulation. Be faithful unto death and I will give to you the crown of life' (Rev. 2:10).

What this verse tells us is that God knows everything beforehand and that nothing takes Him by surprise. It demonstrates that God is in overall control, not Satan, since it is God who grants Satan permission to instigate our testing and suffering, whether by persecution, illness or misfortune. One only needs to read the story of Job to understand how that one works! Whatever the form of suffering is, we can take great encouragement as we look at the bigger picture of what suffering ultimately leads to. Provided we remain faithful (full of faith) to the point of death, we will receive from Jesus the crown of life. All of this teaches us that God uses our suffering for His purpose and ultimately for our good. It is worth repeating a verse I have already quoted twice before since it is a promise that needs to be engrained on the heart of all who suffer for the sake of Christ:

'And we know that for those who love God all things work together for good, for those who are called according to his purpose' (Rom. 8:28).

The 'good' speaks of a time that relates not so much to this life but to the life to come. This means that we can endure the suffering we encounter in this life by recognizing it as a future blessing. In our walk with Jesus, we are called to suffer many things (1 Peter 2:20–21) and would do well to remember that Jesus Himself learned obedience through what He suffered (Heb. 5:7–9).

Jesus Suffered

'But we see him who for a little while was made lower than the angels, namely Jesus, crowned with glory and honor because of the suffering of death, so that by the grace of God he might taste death for everyone. For it was fitting that he, for whom and by whom all things exist, in bringing many sons to glory, should make the founder of their salvation perfect through suffering' (Heb.2:9–10).

Whenever I face the question of why God allows His beloved children to suffer so badly, I have to remind myself that God allowed His Son Jesus to suffer more than any other human who has ever lived. Over the course of human history, millions of soldiers have left their families and homes to suffer the brutal and horrific warfare on the front line of the bloody battlefield. The suffering of Jesus began when He left the glory of heaven in order to become one of us in this fallen world. He took Himself to the frontline of the bloody battlefield of the cross, where He willingly suffered the brutality of Roman execution by crucifixion. Jesus took Himself to that deadly battlefront to win the battle of our souls, not to provide us with a temporary freedom, but an eternal redemption.

The excruciating physical and mental agony of crucifixion meant that Jesus experienced the most unbearable pain anyone has endured. Having already suffered the terrible pain of Roman flogging which ripped open His flesh, the worst pain was yet to come as He was nailed to the cross. Throughout it all, He underwent the psychological pain of public humiliation, rejection, injustice and hatred. While all of this sounds bad enough, Jesus experienced the very worst sorrow at the cross as His Father in heaven turned His back on Him. In this way, Jesus suffered the full impact of His Father's wrath. Speaking of this event, the Prophet Isaiah prophesied in the 8th-century BC:

> '*He was despised and rejected by men, a man of sorrows and acquainted with grief; and as one from whom men hide their faces he was despised, and we esteemed him not. Surely he has borne our griefs and carried our sorrows; yet we esteemed him stricken, smitten by God, and afflicted. But he was pierced for our transgressions; He was crushed for our iniquities; upon him was the chastisement that brought us peace, and with his wounds we are healed'* (Isa. 53:3–5).

Was Jesus punished by God and did God cause Him to suffer? Yes, more than we can ever know. There are Christians who cannot bring themselves to accept such a thing, labelling it as cosmic child abuse. However, I do not think Jesus saw Himself as such a victim, as the following verse reveals in Hebrews 12:2–3:

> '*...looking to Jesus, the founder and perfecter of our faith, who for the joy that was set before him endured the cross, despising the shame, and is seated at the right hand of the throne of God.*'

In His human form, Jesus knows what it feels like to suffer the worst of all punishments. He has been there Himself, which means that He is more than qualified to identify with us in all of our pain and suffering. Did God want to punish His only Son and make Him suffer? Yes, but not because of anything Jesus had done, but because of what we have done. Therefore, God does not want to punish me or make me suffer, because Jesus has taken the full consequences of my sin committed against God upon Himself. Not only that, but Jesus has imputed to me the blessing of His righteousness and perfection, so that I may stand before God justified and blameless:

'For our sake He [God] *made him to be sin who knew no sin, so that in him we might become the righteousness of God'* (2 Cor. 5:21).

If Jesus only saw His life from a human perspective, He could have reasoned that His punishment and suffering to be grossly unfair and unjust. Yet Jesus looked beyond His suffering, seeing the bigger picture of what His suffering was going to achieve. We, too, must look past our suffering that seeks to tell us that God is punishing us and wants us to suffer. Like Jesus, we must look beyond our suffering in this life, to the joy set before us that God, in His love and care, has kept for us in heaven.

Prayer Does Not Work

Perhaps God cannot heal me because prayer does not work. Faith and prayer go hand in hand since prayer is an expression of faith. I have prayed my socks off, praying from every perceivable angle. I have asked, begged and pleaded, yet in spite of all those Scriptures which appear to promise my healing, I have received no healing. In my times of solitude with God, I have exhausted myself of all words with which to pray, left with nothing more but to weep in His presence, yet my cries continue to go unanswered.

In the world of reality, which is where I live, I do not see God answering our really big prayers. This immediately puts my faith to the test. It is very easy to say that God healed my back pain, found me a new job or a parking space, but these are things that could have happened anyway. These do not *prove* that God has intervened or that the miraculous hand of God was most definitely at work, by-passing the laws of nature. That being said, the sudden unexplainable removal of every cancer cell from within my body would prove beyond any reasonable doubt that God has stepped in and intervened. I ask; What good reason does God have to deny Himself much honour and glory by demonstrating supernatural power and authority over the fallen natural realm?

When something works out the way we have been praying, we give thanks to God as we honour Him for a positive outcome. We thank Him for the blessings of His goodness, kindness and protection that we receive each new day. Nevertheless, when things go seriously wrong and our really big prayers remain unanswered, our confidence in prayer is deeply undermined.

The point I am trying to make is this. If my God-honouring prayers for healing were answered, both my faith, my wife's faith and the faith of the church would be greatly bolstered and encouraged, especially in the area of witness. In light of this, I struggle in my natural self to comprehend why God doesn't comply! However, my spiritual self tells me that I need to accept what the Apostle Paul said: *'for we walk by faith, not by sight'* (2 Cor. 5:7).

Does Paul's teaching make faith or prayer any easier? No. What it does do is establish the need for my faith to be firmly embedded in what Christ has *already* accomplished at the cross. I am reminded of the time when Jesus spent His last night in the Garden of Gethsemane. There He earnestly prayed to God His Father for the next day's crucifixion to pass Him by. Jesus prayed for God to *'remove this cup from me,'* yet that request went unanswered (Mark 14:36 & Luke 22:42). Considering what was at stake, together with the implications that would have arisen had God answered Jesus's request, this was surely the biggest prayer request ever presented to God. However, Jesus made His request adding the words *'not my will but yours be done.'* God answered the prayer of Jesus by carrying out His will, to which Jesus wholly surrendered Himself. The obedience and acceptance of Jesus to carry out His Father's will is staggering. At any point in time, Jesus could have changed His mind and in some supernatural way, released Himself from the nails that held Him to the cross. Instead, Jesus kept Himself there in spite of the taunts by those who looked on:

"You who would destroy the temple and rebuild it in three days, save yourself! If you are the Son of God, come down from the cross!" So also the chief priests, with the scribes and elders, mocked him, saying, "He saved others; He cannot save himself. He is the King of Israel; let him come down now from the cross, and we will believe in him. He trusts in God; let God deliver him now, if He desires him. For He said, 'I am the Son of God'" (Matt. 27:40–43).

Can you imagine how tempting it must have been for Jesus to prove them all wrong and grant their mocking request by stepping down from the cross? Can you imagine the look of disbelief and embarrassment on their faces? Yet Jesus knew that such an impressive display would have robbed Him of what God had called for Him to accomplish. The time is coming when Jesus will be vindicated globally, coming down not from the cross but out of heaven at His second coming:

'Behold, He is coming with the clouds, and every eye will see him, even those who pierced him, and all tribes of the earth will wail on account of him' (Rev. 1:7).

Does prayer work? Yes, but not in the way that we would like it to. To understand how prayer works, we need to look at what the deeper point of prayer is.

Chapter 30

WHAT IS THE DEEPER POINT OF PRAYER?

So many prayers prayed time after time and so many angles explored from which to pray. At what point does God hear our prayer, the first time or the hundredth time? How many times do I need to pray the same thing over and over again before God decides to give my prayer His attention?

There have been many times when I no longer had the ability to speak or pray words. Instead, I re-commit all the words I have already prayed and simply leave those words with God and wait upon Him in silent surrender. My silence is often broken by the sound of my weeping that expresses my sense of helplessness and total resignation. As I consider the many ongoing unanswered prayers that both I and the church have continued to pray, I wonder what worth, meaning and significance they all have? It was in my Desert that I came to the understanding that the crucial point of prayer is that it develops and validates my unconditional trust in God. Prayer is simply the demonstration and expression of my trust in His sovereign will. It is to seek first the kingdom of God and pray, '*Your kingdom come, your will be done.*'

My starting point in prayer is to pray from a position of knowing that God always hears me, trusting in the sovereignty of God that He will always bring to pass His will, no matter what the outcome. I pray from a position that knows that I cannot dictate to God what His will ought to be or stop Him from carrying out what He has already decided to do. By the will of God, I am either afflicted with cancer or protected from cancer. By the will of God, I am either healed or not healed. Do I always understand His will? No, but that is what trust is all about. Trust is to trust when I do not understand, and my trouble makes no sense to me whatsoever. The agony of the Desert Place did not really teach me *what* to pray, although that was really important, but the *position* of trust from which to pray.

If prayer means anything at all, I have to believe that God is responsible for withholding my healing and that He is doing so for a reason. For sure, my illness is providing me with a tremendous opportunity to bear witness to the sufficiency of Jesus. Even so, I continue to pray that the day will come when my healing will serve His purposes *more* than my illness. Does this mean I am to sweep all of those Scriptures that appear to promise my healing under the carpet? How do I get them to make sense without twisting their meaning on contradicting them? All of those Scriptures were written to encourage, not discourage. For those Scriptures to make any sense and hold any kind of validity, I need to interpret them in the light of other Scriptures and allow Scripture to interpret Scripture. I especially need to interpret those healing and asking verses in light of the following verse:

> '*And this is the confidence that we have toward him, that if we ask anything according to his will he hears us. And if we know that he hears us in whatever we ask, we know that we have the requests that we have asked of him*'
> (1 John 5:14–15).

This verse teaches me that God will grant my requests if my request is in accordance with His will, giving me the confidence that my prayer will certainly be answered. The prayer that accords with God's will is the only prayer that God listens to and responds to. God hears His will being prayed and He answers to His will. If this interpretation is correct, I have to apply the principles of this verse to all of the other Scriptures relating to prayer mentioned above. This is an obvious case of Scripture interpreting Scripture, rather than Scripture contradicting itself.

While God continues to withhold my healing, I nevertheless continue to persist in prayer like the story of the persistent

208

widow's request to the unjust judge (Luke 18:1–8). I do this knowing that I cannot tell God what to do, no matter how sincere or passionate my prayers might be. God is not my genie; He is my sovereign. My faith in Christ is not based upon God healing me of cancer, but upon His atoning work accomplished at the cross. It was there where Jesus healed me of my spiritual disease and the eternal consequences that come with that horrific condition. My faith lies firmly in Christ and not in the blessings He supplies or withholds. My faith is firmly grounded and established in the one blessing that comes from what Christ accomplished at the cross and the blessing of my eternal salvation.

Let me ask you a question. In spite of all the praying for God's blessing and favour to rest upon you, what if everything in your life was taken away; what kind of faith would you be left with? I can tell you for certain, that what *kind* of faith you have would soon become apparent. Unless our faith and trust in Jesus is bigger than everything else in our life, we will fail to comprehend the sufficiency of God's grace and His eternal favour and blessing that rests upon us in Christ.

Whenever I pray, I do so as one who is fully convinced that Jesus saves me from the condemnation of my sins. I also pray, fully convinced that if He wanted to heal me of terminal cancer, He would. All power and authority in heaven and on earth has been given to Him, and He has the power and the authority to heal or not to heal. For my own satisfaction, I see prayer as the expression and demonstration of my full dependency on Christ, whatever I happen to be praying for. In this way, prayer *always* works.

Chapter 31

THE SOVEREIGNTY OF GOD

Faith Trusts in the Sovereignty of God

I hope that by now I have given a satisfactory answer to some of my own big questions, such as: What does a real faith look like? How do I connect my faith to my prayers? Why doesn't God answer my big prayers?

All of these questions lead to the same answer, which demands that I trust in the sovereignty of God. Through trust, we learn to ask, surrender and wait to see what God's Sovereign will determines. I have no idea if God will heal me or not. This 'not knowing' requires more of my trust than if I did know. My ability to trust in God says nothing about me. I cannot claim any credit for trusting in God. My trust does not rest in my own reasoning or assumptions but in the word of God and what that word tells me about the faithfulness and trustworthiness of Jesus. It is not about me; it is all about Jesus. My ability to trust says nothing about me, but everything about who Jesus is. When someone is sovereign, they possess supreme power and authority over the realm in which they reign. God is sovereign over the whole of history and all of creation. Everything is subject to His sovereignty, be it in the physical or spiritual realm. How does God make sure that everything He wills to happen actually happens, and everything He does not will to happen does not happen? I have no idea whatsoever!

Wrestling with God's Sovereignty

If I were sovereign, I would grant myself immediate and total healing for the sake of my family. I would grant myself immediate and total healing for the sake of providing the church with such a powerful witness. Why doesn't God think the same way I do? I can think of numerous people who might possibly put their faith in Jesus and escape the clutches of hell as the result of such a powerful witness. So why doesn't God go ahead and heal me; what could go wrong?

Often when we pray, we find ourselves wrestling with the sovereignty of God. Needless to say, the sovereignty of God puts our faith to the test. When we pray, our faith is being examined, pruned, refined and stretched as we learn to trust in God's wisdom rather than our own. When we pray, we learn to trust in God's sovereignty because He *always* does what is right. It is this trust that gives me a rest and a peace that is not of this world.

Chapter 32

THE TESTING OF MY WIFE'S FAITH

The truth is, my predicament is no different to that of an elderly Christian in their late seventies, whose health is showing signs of wear and tear. Both of us know that we are closer to death than we have ever been before. Both of us could take a sudden turn for the worse. However, both of us know that the end is just the beginning of a glorious future in the presence of Christ. In that case, what is so different about me dying from terminal cancer and an elderly Christian on their deathbed who has been blessed with an abundance of years? The difficulty to be struggled with is the question of timing.

For one thing, as I write, I am only 57 years old, and my wife is just 47. We have two children who are only in their late teens or early twenties. Through the bond of marriage, we have been made one and shared together the many blessings that God has bestowed upon us both. Today we find ourselves sharing in the same trial that God has allowed to come our way. The testing of my faith has by association tested the faith of my wife. It is a sobering thought to know that none of us gets to choose what kind of trial God grants to come our way. Although we both vowed 'for better or worse', the trial we face today is not what Krissie signed up for when we first became husband and wife.

Throughout our years of marriage, Krissie has stood by me all the way. Her whole identity has been wrapped up in being my wife, the mother of our children and creating a family home and way of life. She has proved to be so faithful in supporting me during my three years at theological college, a time she found to be extremely difficult. She has proved so faithful to my calling, which took us away from our family home and the place that had been the best

212

and happiest time of our lives. She has proved to be so faithful, loyal and supportive during the whole of my first five years in ministry, taking an active role in the life of the church and playing her part.

During all my stays at the Royal Marsden and the National Hospital of Neurology at Queen Square, Krissie commuted into London every day to sit by the side of my bed. At the end of the day, she made her way back home, and no matter how hard I tried, I could not persuade her to give herself a much-needed rest by staying home. Instead, she came, and she sat. In all of these things, she has stood by me, loved me, supported me, been there for me and cared for me. She has never abandoned me or been unfaithful. She has been faithful throughout, while at the same time, her faith in God is being put to the test.

Both of us have been so grateful that the church has provided us with a four-bedroomed detached manse. As good as this is and as strange as this might sound, we have never considered the manse to be our home. When most people move home, they get to choose the exact location they live in and the character of a house that suits their personal tastes and preferences. They decorate the house so that it feels like home and has their stamp on it. It is difficult to do that with a manse since it is owned by the church and the period of occupancy is unknown. I am the one whom God has called into this place of ministry, but my wife was not, and in one sense, she has had to make more of a sacrifice than I have.

Mourning What has Already Been Lost

While we share in the same suffering of today, we suffer in different ways. We both lost our normal way of life the moment I started theological college. That normality was buried even deeper the moment we left Devon to come London way. Whatever normality we have tried to create while living here, it has now been taken away by the predicament of my serious illness. As a result, Krissie has lost what she was looking forward to in our future years, such as growing old together, celebrating at least 50 years of marriage while watching Lucy and James make a life for themselves, and who knows, grandchildren!

Although I am still here, Krissie has lost the man she once married. I am not the same person I once was. Over the last two years, I have aged in appearance by at least 20 years due to the radiotherapy to my brain. I do not have the energy or spark I once had and often feel fatigued and subdued because of my lethargy and heavy eyelids. I am no longer allowed to drive, which means that I rely on Krissie to drive me around. In all of this, Krissie has become my carer, and I the patient.

As hard as she has tried, Krissie struggles to work out where God is in all of this. Unable to make any acceptable sense of it, she gets those moments when she feels as though God is punishing her. She feels cheated and cannot understand why God, who is omniscient, took us away from our happy home in Devon whilst knowing how difficult her life was going to become. Considering the significant sacrifices that we have made in order to step out in obedience to God's calling, Krissie struggles to reason why God would repay us in such a way. All of God's blessings in the past now seem to have been cancelled out by the curse of today. I have tried to encourage her to look at the bigger picture and to see that the curse of today will be cancelled out by the greatest ever blessing which is yet to come. However, that anticipated future joy in the kingdom of God seems so far removed from the trials of today, which speak far louder and have a much more powerful voice.

I have found it very difficult to witness the impact this trial is having upon my wife. I feel incredibly helpless, and my feeble efforts to comfort her amount to nothing. I get to see first-hand how much my wife is hurting as she tries her best to deal with her confusion, fear and regrets. I know that each day she struggles to hold back the tears, suppressing the anguish that lies just beneath the surface. I cannot stand in the place of God and attempt to justify what He allows or disallows and have no easy answers that will satisfy my wife. The best I can offer is to listen. Today, my overriding prayer for Krissie is that God would heal me, since it seems to me that this is the only thing that would speak into her life and make any real sense.

What About Lucy and James?

As I write (Sept 2017), our children are no longer fully compliant, sweet, innocent infants. Anyone who has teenage children knows how impossible it is to be the same influential parent that you once were. That influence has greatly dwindled in their teenage years as we have found ourselves in competition with the enticing influence of the attractive world outside. Unless you have managed to wrap up your teenage children in cotton wool or locked them up in the cellar free from anything that is media-driven, you face an almost impossible task. Most of the time, we parents try to make sense of this battle by convincing ourselves that our teenagers are on a voyage of necessary discovery as they struggle to work out who they really are in the world of today.

Since moving away from Devon, during what were very formative years for them both, they have been forced to make big adaptions to their young lives. They came with a very good basic understanding of the well-known Bible stories and why they need Jesus. Raising young children into the Christian faith is very easy and straightforward, but once they start growing and begin to discover what the world has to offer, it is a totally different story. They begin to recognize that most people are not Christians and do not go to church. The new friends they make have no clue about the Christian faith, prompting them to sense that perhaps mum and dad are a bit quirky and out of touch with reality. In the last seven years, both Lucy and James have shown little interest in matters of faith. Rather, they have developed a far greater pull towards the appeal of the exciting world 'out there'. This is going to be a legitimate worry for any Christian parent who is concerned about their children's salvation. Since March 2016, this concern has been heightened as Lucy and James have had to take on board the reality of my diagnosis and its future implications for them.

As a heating engineer back in Devon, I had a lot more leisure time which meant we had more time to do things together as a family, especially at the weekends. This is in stark contrast to that of working as a pastor. For example, having just one day off each week takes its toll on family life. However, with the passing of times and seasons, the dynamics of family life would have inevitably changed, regardless of where we lived.

The biggest concern for Krissie and myself is the impact my death would have on Lucy and James's perception of God. My prayer for both of them is the same prayer I pray for Krissie; that God would show them His mercy and compassion by completely healing and restoring me. I ask this prayer because my healing would provide them with such a powerful witness that would surely captivate their attention to the reality of God's power and presence, paving the way for their salvation. In this sense, their salvation is in God's hands because my healing is in God's hands. I continue to pray that God will draw them to Jesus, guiding them to a place in their lives where they will understand that their greatest need in life is to get right with God. Faith is so very personal; I cannot pass my faith on to anyone, but I wish I could make my children an exception. I love them so dearly and they mean everything to me.

Chapter 33

MINISTRY WITH CANCER

Some might think that I should have stepped down from ministry the moment I was diagnosed; after all, how can I possibly be fit for purpose and have the right frame of mind to carry on ministering to others?

Even though I have multiple cancers in my brain and body, I am still able to function well enough to do what I can. I hope that what I have done is enough to make a difference and that I have been of some benefit. The last thing I want to be is a liability. The cancer drugs have worked well enough, keeping the cancer under control, although I am convinced that they affect my ability to concentrate. My appetite has been restored and I have regained the three stone that I had lost. That being said, I face a constant battle. In December 2016, my brain triggered a seizure that lasted 30 minutes, so I added seizure tablets to my list of other tablets. There are many times when I feel dazed, drowsy, spaced out, fatigued and unsteady, sending me into a state of silence and the need to shut down inside my own shell. At such times, my bed becomes a place of refuge. On these occasions, I am forced to recognize my complete state of helplessness before God, and I question how much longer I can carry on in ministry.

A significant obstacle to my ministry has been the onset of ocular myasthenia gravis, which makes it difficult to read, prepare and present sermons. In one sense, the easiest thing for me to do would be to step down from ministry. I have often struggled with this dilemma, wondering if the church will make this choice for me. My top priority is to be faithful to the ministry that God has called me to. I know that I can only carry on so long as God still wants me to, relying on Him to give me His voice, without which,

I have no voice, and I no longer want to continue in ministry. There have been times during the last year when I have made the short walk on Sunday mornings from the manse to the church next door, wanting to turn back. At times, that walk has been difficult since I have not felt up to the task in hand or feel that I possess the mental capacity to get through the service. However, I still sense the calling of God to this place of ministry.

Taking the Church with Me

Throughout my ministry, my aim has been to lead the church by example, always pointing to Jesus, who is my life, hope, peace, security, joy and future. I do not have the power to do this unless I possess a faith that is given strength by the sufficiency of God's grace. I have determined to take the church with me on this journey of authentic faith that proves its authenticity as it is lived out in the reality of a fallen body and a fallen world. I recognize this moment in time to be the most significant season of my ministry, yet I would never choose to have it this way, far from it. The earthly man in me would much rather settle down to a less demanding ministry.

Preaching with Cancer

I have always considered my call into ministry to fulfil the commission that God had called me to. The call is for the church to get rid of her casual and complacent Christianity and to spiritually wake up, grow up and love God with all. That is simple, right? Maintaining the status quo has never been an option, either for the church or the individual. I know that God has not called me to entertain, be popular or liked. God has not called me to tell people what they want to hear or promote myself or my own ideas or to amuse people but to promote and teach what God says through the truth of the whole counsel of His word. I preach with confidence in God's word because of the powerful effect it had on me all those years ago in the Desert. I have experienced for myself the transformational power of God's word in the Bible, and I know that anyone who seeks after God diligently through its pages will find what I have found.

Consequently, I have tried to get across to the church the importance of taking God seriously and to get rid of all the superficial, shallow faith that makes people feel comfortable. I have tried to take the church out of a basic Sunday school theology and into a curiosity that explores a deeper, richer, mature theology that is found within the pages of Scripture. One church member told me that they wanted to keep their faith simple, yet even the simplest of faith still requires a radical change to one's life and mindset. As I desire an authentic faith for myself, I aim to present an authentic faith to the church. I want to encourage each member of the church to think things through, deeply and biblically for themselves.

This does not make for popular, funny or entertaining preaching, and I dare say there are those who listen to my preaching and wish I would lighten up and crack a few jokes. This though is not what God has called me to, and I am certain that when I stand before Jesus, He will not condemn me for not entertaining the crowd or making people laugh. Instead, I want to hear Him say:

'Well done, good and faithful servant. You have been faithful over a little; I will set you over much. Enter into the joy of your master' (Matt. 25:21).

God has not called me to a ministry that seeks to take the church through the wide and easy way, but through the narrow gate and along the hard way that leads to abundant life in Christ. In my preaching, I have tried to encourage each member of the church not to limit themselves to the sands of shallow water, where they are happy to remain in spiritual infancy with their bucket and spade. Authentic faith demands we go into deeper water and learn to swim, getting to grips with theology, doctrine and a deeper biblical understanding of the character and nature of God. It is in the deeper waters where we learn to swim against the dangerous currents of living life in the real world. This takes effort and discipline as we live out our witness and testimony in a world that is hostile towards Christianity. This is the world where Jesus commands His followers to pick up their cross and follow Him (Matt. 10:38 & Luke 14:27).

I have never sought to preach an easy message, and preaching with terminal cancer has further empowered me to preach a serious message that takes God seriously and does not allow me to focus my preaching on a lighthearted, playschool type Christianity. It is to preach of both the goodness and severity of God, His love and judgment, heaven and hell. It is to preach of the serious consequences of sin and the joy of forgiveness. Too many Christians who were converted many years ago do not seem to realize that God still needs to perform His ongoing sanctifying work in them, a necessary work that puts to death the desires of their old sinful nature and conform them into the likeness of Jesus. The truth is, every follower of Jesus needs a complete overhaul, a demolition job that does away with all of our worldly desires and self-righteousness. Every Christian needs to be constantly refined, pruned and challenged, so that they continue to bear and grow the good fruit that is produced from abiding in Jesus, who taught His disciples:

'I am the true vine, and my Father is the vinedresser. Every branch in me that does not bear fruit he takes away, and every branch that does bear fruit he prunes, that it may bear more fruit' (John 15:1–2).

Needless to say, the whole counsel of God revealed in the Scriptures has at its core the incredibly good news that is Jesus Christ, who once said: *'For my yoke is easy and my burden is light'* (Matt. 11:30), yet the same Jesus also said:

'If anyone comes to me and does not hate his own father and mother and wife and children and brothers and sisters, yes, and even his own life, he cannot be my disciple' (Luke 14:26).

The verses above seem to contradict each other, yet they do not. Preaching the truth of God's word needs to be balanced, and the only way to do that is to preach the whole counsel of God as written in the Bible. My illness is helping me to serve that purpose as I preach from a platform of suffering, together with the joy of my salvation.

How Long?

I have always said that I'm not hanging on to ministry just to see how long I can last the distance. When the right time comes, I know that I will no longer want to remain in ministry. I remain in ministry since I do not see this terminal cancer either as an accident or a mistake. Does God ever make mistakes? The predicament of my illness has given to me a greater opportunity to bear witness to my salvation and the sufficiency of God's grace. Even when the walk on Sundays from the manse to the church building has been a difficult one, when the moment came to stand at the lectern to preach, my illness has never restricted my ability to do so. As I continue to serve the church in this way, I am aware that God sometimes permits or even ordains suffering so that we can serve Him better. The Apostle Paul writes:

> *'So to keep me from becoming conceited because of the surpassing greatness of the revelation, a thorn was given me in the flesh, a messenger of Satan to harass me, to keep me from becoming conceited. Three times I pleaded with the Lord about this, that it should leave me. But He said to me, "My grace is sufficient for you, for my power is made perfect in weakness." Therefore I will boast all the more gladly of my weaknesses, so that the power of Christ may rest upon me'* (2 Cor. 12:7–9).

It is through my weaknesses that I am trusting in the strength of God to keep me in ministry. God could have taken me by now, but He has not, and so I remain. While I remain, I do not pretend that everything is normal and that it is business as usual. By the end of 2017, the church will have endured nearly two years of having a pastor who is not up to scratch. I often wonder if the patience of the church might possibly be wearing thin, giving way to a growing restlessness that desires to pave the way for a new beginning. Only this morning I read how Jesus taught His disciples to pray:

'If you then, who are evil, know how to give good gifts to your children, how much more will the heavenly Father give the Holy Spirit to those who ask him!' (Luke 11:13).

I continue to ask for that good gift of the Holy Spirit to enable me to carry on, while at the same time asking for the Spirit to compel me when to stop.

Chapter 34

ONE DAY AT A TIME

With all of the uncertainty that my situation creates, I have learnt to put into practice a valuable lesson I first learnt in the Desert Place. That lesson is to take one day at a time. I came out of the Desert thinking that nothing would surprise me anymore, since what I had previously thought could never happen, did happen. The Desert proved that life is full of surprises, and none of us knows what might happen tomorrow. None of us has a right to still be alive tomorrow, although we so often live as though we do.

Sometimes we live days when life feels good, full of promise and hope. Yet, as rewarding as those days might be, none of them has the power to cancel out the arrival of our last and final day. Even our best day cannot save us, which might even turn out to be our last. While nations rise and nations fall, so too, generations come and generations go, along with each day. Nothing is as stable as we would like to imagine, and everything is far more fragile than we would like to accept. Each new day I wake to be reminded that I am on death row, awaiting my execution by cancer. No amount of positive thinking, well-wishers or sunshiny days can change this fact of reality. I am satisfied to accept that the numbers of my days are entirely in the hands of God. If I have any say in the matter, it is that God takes me home to be with Him once I am of no benefit to anyone. There are times when I sense that I have reached that place, times when I feel as though I am a lousy husband, father and pastor all at the same time. In such moments, I cry out for God to take me home. Nevertheless, each new morning my first waking thought is that God has given to me the beginning of a new day. He could have taken me in the night, but He did not. This new day is a gift from God, and I begin it knowing that it could be my last. This is the same predicament for all of us.

There is only one way to face each new day, and that is to face it as one who is in Christ. In Him, I face no condemnation and am full of hope. In Christ, I can face the day rejoicing in the salvation I have in Him. In Christ, I face the day looking at the bigger eternal picture, which puts everything into its correct perspective. In Christ, I can face the day knowing that no one day lasts forever. The sun rises to give birth to the light of a fresh new day, and a short time later sets to allow the darkness of night to bring that day to an end. Each day cannot last and must end. We begin life in the light of the dawning of physical birth, and we end life through the darkness of physical death. Nevertheless, the one who is in Christ has already experienced the dawning of a new day, a new birth and a new life that follows in the eternal footsteps of the one who has gone before us: Jesus. This new day is everlasting and will never end, for not even physical death can bring it to an end but rather serves the purpose of opening the doorway into the eternal kingdom of God.

Wanting to Go

I look around at the happiness people strive to obtain in this life. As I look at faces that reveal a beautiful smile and the sound of laughter, I see something that brings me great sadness. This is because I know what the outcome of their happiness without God is leading to. I fail to share in their happiness that is happy to live without God. As someone whom Jesus has saved from his sin, I ought to be far happier than those who do not believe in Jesus, yet I have to confess that I am not. How can this be? Is my faith not working properly? Paul wrote:

> '*But our citizenship is in heaven, and we eagerly await a Saviour from there, the Lord Jesus Christ*'(Philippians 3:20).

I fail to share in the same happiness as those who have no faith because all of their happiness is placed in this world, which is fragile and temporary. Since they believe in nothing else, this world is all they have, and it is where they belong. As a citizen of heaven, I know that I do not belong to or fit in with this world. I live as some kind of stranger or alien, a fugitive in a foreign land far away from my true home. I do not feel comfortable, secure or settled in this foreign land since I am surrounded by the ugliness of sin and am separated from the tangible presence of God.

Does this mean that I am to live an unhappy life until I get to heaven, where everything is blissfully happy? No! Through my faith in Jesus, I can live this life with a profound sense of joy that speaks of contentment and delight that only comes through knowing where my true home is, and that I am heading in that direction and will one day arrive. This is why I do not share in the happiness that others have, because the source of their happiness and my happiness are built upon two very different foundations. The Apostle Paul wrote:

'For we know that if the tent that is our earthly home is destroyed, we have a building from God, a house not made with hands, eternal in the heavens. For in this tent we groan, longing to put on our heavenly dwelling' (2 Cor. 5:1–2).

Even though I constantly live in the joy of my salvation, there are times when I become aggrieved with living in a fallen world and a fallen body. I am fed up with living in a godless world whose god and ruler is the Devil. I am fed up of living in a world where I am surrounded by the presence of sin with all of its ghastly destructive consequences.

In spite of all the best efforts by various governments, social organizations and church movements who endeavour to make this world a happier place, they are on a road to nowhere since their efforts are powerless to remove humanities fallen condition and alienation from God. The only solution is to be reconciled to God through Christ. It is only through this reconciliation that true happiness, lasting joy and peace can ever be realized in this life.

This world can never enjoy such a utopia until Jesus returns to establish His righteous kingdom on earth.

Wanting to Stay

I live within a paradox: On the one hand, I want to go and be with the Lord, while on the other, I want to stay. I do not want to leave Krissie on her own for obvious reasons, yet there is another reason I want to stay. I do not ask God to miraculously heal me just so that I can add another 15 years to my life; I ask so that I may be given more opportunity to bear witness to my healing, using it as a supernatural platform from which to do the work of an evangelist and proclaim the gospel message of salvation in Jesus to those who need to hear. My healing is not to serve myself but the kingdom of God, but once I leave this life, I will have no more opportunity to do so.

The mandate that disciples of Jesus live with is to bear witness to Him within this fallen realm. It is a world that is not interested in what we proclaim and is likely to consider us to be abnormal, unreasonable, irrational, divisive and offensive. We are considered to be ignorant of the facts, gullible, intolerant and foolish, a strange archaic people whose message is way out of sync with the sophistication and enlightenment that the world of today lives in. The time is fast approaching, when to bear witness to Jesus is going to cost, making us extremely unpopular since the Jesus of the Bible, who we represent, stands in opposition to what the culture of today deems to be acceptable, beneficial and progressive.

Although what I believe makes perfect sense to me and sounds totally reasonable and sane, what I represent will soon be deemed unacceptable. It is only a matter of time before the church will be forced to fall in line to accept and endorse secular liberal ideologies that are being woven into every fabric of society. The time is coming when living out a life of faithful witness to Christ will not only be difficult but dangerous and costly. Freedom of speech is under attack, and unless both the individual and the

226

church are prepared to pick up their cross and follow in the footsteps of Jesus, they will be silenced. Jesus once said:

> *'For what does it profit a man if he gains the whole world and loses or forfeits himself? For whoever is ashamed of me and my words, of him will the Son of Man be ashamed when he comes in his glory and the glory of the Father and the holy angels'* (Luke 9:25–26).

The Apostle Paul writes:

> *'For I am not ashamed of the gospel, for it is the power of God for salvation to everyone who believes, to the Jew first and also to the Greek'* (Rom. 1:16).

Like Paul, the faithful follower of Christ will need to exercise a faith that is bold and courageous, yet this is what Christ has called each one of His disciples into; a mission of faithful endurance and proclamation of the true gospel that might literally cost the disciple everything that they have. Yet Jesus has given to us this promise:

> *'If anyone loves me, he will keep my word, and my Father will love him, and we will come to him and make our home with him'* (John 14:23).

Just before Jesus ascended back into heaven after rising from the dead, He told His disciples:

> *'Go therefore and make disciples of all nations, baptizing them in the name of the Father and of the Son and of the Holy Spirit, teaching them to observe all that I have commanded you. And behold, I am with you always, to the end of the age'* (Matt. 28:19–20).

Chapter 35

WAITING UPON GOD

The approach of 1 January 2018 proved to be a tense time. I had set out to pray that the arrival of the New Year would see the arrival of my healing and a new ministry to go with it. I have always believed that the moment I became aware that my eyes have been fully restored to what they should be, this was a sure sign that God has eradicated every single cancerous cell from within my body and brain. On 31 December 2017, I fasted and prayed that I would wake up on New Year's morning with a new pair of eyes. Alas, I woke up with the same pair of eyes.

On Friday, 27 September 2019, my scan results revealed that some of the existing tumours had started to grow slightly alongside two new tumours, meaning that I was no longer stable and that the tide had now begun to turn. The consultants told me that this was a significant change because it revealed that the dabrafenib medication was no longer keeping the cancer under control. I was told by the Marsden that they could do no more and were handing me over to the palliative care of a hospice. I was told that my life expectancy was now between one to six months, depending on how aggressive the cancers proved to be. However, by the following Monday, Krissie had persuaded the Marsden to put me back on the medication since it might at least slow down the advancing cancer. Consequently, I was placed back under the Marsden's care and continue with the daily routine of taking medication and undergoing MRI and CT scans every eight weeks.

In the lead up to Christmas 2019, the strain of ministry with cancer was taking its toll, and I became convinced that I was no longer fit for purpose. In January 2020, along came Covid-19, followed in March by lockdown. Like most other churches, WBC met via zoom, signalling the end of my public ministry. To compensate, I sent out daily blogs to the church which lasted for 100 days. Shortly after, I sent out an additional blog in which I explained to the church that I had got to the point where my mind and body were saying 'enough'.

I have been on long-term sick leave since July 2020, and on November 10th we moved out of the manse and into a new home in Reigate. This is a move that prepares Krissie for a future without me, and I am grateful that the Lord has allowed me to see her begin to settle down into her new home. It is now April 2021, and another year is well underway. I feel increasingly unsettled on at least two counts. Firstly, I am tired of living in a fallen body which I now deem to be more of a burden and nuisance to others rather than a blessing. Secondly, I am tired of living in a fallen world that I don't belong to or fit in with. I am weary of living in a world where I am constantly reminded that I am surrounded by the presence of sin and its hideous consequences. I am grieved by the perceived acceptable norm, which is to live independently of God and therefore Godless and Christless. Yet it is to this fallen, alienated, lost world that I have a desire to do the work of an evangelist, to proclaim the precious knowledge of salvation in Jesus Christ to those who need to hear and are willing to listen. However, this appears to be an impossibility since I am not fit for such a purpose; my body is as good as dead, and I am frustrated by my inability to do want I want to do. Needless to say, I have always prayed for my family and their salvation, but now I see this as my sole ministry and the reason why God keeps me here.

CONCLUSION

For over five years, I and others have prayed many prayers for my healing. I know that my prayers will not be answered just because I have used the right persuasive words or methods. The only position I can pray from is my faith in Christ, which is actually very simple. I simply believe that God is sovereign; He does no wrong and is supreme in all wisdom, power and authority. He is always in control, and I can trust Him entirely, and I am content with that. No matter how hard I might try, I cannot gain that contentment by trying to figure everything out for myself. I continue to pray, surrender, abide and wait, while the rest is up to God. It is in this contentment that I find rest and peace. Job declares:

'Though he slay me, I will hope in him' (Job 13:15).

When we are afflicted with times of severe testing and feel totally powerless, God has not failed to protect us. We are not victims but always victors in Christ who remain incredibly blessed by God.

The battle I fight is not against cancer; that battle is in God's hands, and for Him, it is no battle at all.

My faith does not answer all of my questions, let alone the questions of others. Neither do I understand how everything fits together. I have no idea how God works it all out and it is not my responsibility to know. My responsibility and witness is to trust in God, no matter how things look or feel. I do not have to make sense of everything in order to remain faithful to Christ in both life and death.

As I write, the entire world is being held in the grip of fear by Covid-19 and all of its variants, something I believe to be a sure sign of God's 'warning' judgment upon the face of the earth and a time of testing for the church. A time of judgment because of the increase in unrighteousness and rebellion against God (as in the days of Noah – Gen. 6:5–18) and a time of testing that calls for the church to set herself apart, resist compromise with the world and to stand up and proclaim the Gospel of Jesus to a world that is heading for destruction. For the church, this is a timely reminder that this life is lived in preparation for the next, where those who believe in Jesus will appear before His judgment seat and are rewarded for their faithful service to Him done while in the body. (1 Cor. 3:13 – 2 Cor. 5:10 – Eph. 2:10). Having already received the inheritance that comes with salvation, the believer in Christ will reap the benefit from the treasure they have stored up in heaven while living on the earth. With this in mind, I live in the satisfaction that I can never earn my way into heaven and do not even deserve to be there. I live in the comforting knowledge that my salvation is made possible only by what Jesus accomplished through His death and resurrection.

If I had known back in 2010 that I was going to be diagnosed with terminal cancer in 2016, I would have stayed in Devon for the sake of my family. I would not have chosen to put them through all of the instability and uncertainty that they have had to endure because of me. Yet one thing my illness has done is to get me to write what I have written. My writing does not seek to explain everything since there is so much that I do not fully comprehend or understand. As it happens, my writing has turned out to be a biography of my faith and the way that faith has been developed by the different seasons of my life's journey. Writing it has been a beneficial exercise as I have sought to clarify and make sense of my own faith in this messed-up, unpredictable world.

My call for everyone who claims to be a Christian is to stop being so busy, put aside all the distractions that prevent you from thinking too deeply, and begin to seriously examine the faith that you honestly have, not the faith that you claim to have.

More than anything, I hope my writing serves as an ongoing witness to my family of my personal testimony, acting as a lasting legacy to them and through which I continue to speak into their lives long after I am gone.

With nothing else to live for, my aim and purpose each day is to know Christ Jesus, a knowing that solidifies my eternal reconciliation and communion with God. It is a knowing that understands the necessity of dying to my old nature, losing everything this world has to offer, knowing that as I do, I stand to gain everything in Jesus.

I have learnt that what really mattered in ministry was to remain faithful to the ministry that God had called me to, and for that, I am happy to be held accountable to God and no one else.

None of us gets to choose whether we are born into this world or not, but live it we must. Looking back over my life, I can see how faith always works itself out in the practicalities of an unpredictable life. Faith does this knowing the certainty and predictability of its final destiny, which is to live in the fullness of God's presence and goodness in His eternal kingdom. Until any of us arrive there, we must work out our faith in and through every situation that life throws our way, from the day of our birth into the kingdom of God and our final arrival when we get to be with the Lord forever.

Whenever faith seems to be ineffective, we must remind ourselves that faith *always* works because it is placed in Christ who is always stable, secure, solid and unchanging. Faith in faith never works, but faith in God through Jesus always works, both in life and death, because God holds both in His hands. Faith in Christ *always* works, since it is placed in the one who always knows the end from the beginning and who somehow works out everything according to the counsel of His will.

The unpredictability of each new day teaches me to 'trust and obey, for there's no other way.' Faith, and therefore salvation, gets worked out in the unpredictability and messiness of everyday life. Such faith does not insist on me getting my own way but to trust in God having His way. I am not to fit God into my preferences but to allow God to fit me in with His purposes. For the last five years, that trust has paved the way for me to make preparations for the gates of death to usher me into the presence of the Lord!

Each new day, I sense the deep need to abandon myself to Jesus, for in Him, I have everything that I really need. There is something within me that only feels rested and secure as I take refuge in Him, as if to hide myself in Him.

Each new day, my many failings and weaknesses that belong to my sinful nature do not condemn me but rather show up the righteousness that Christ has imputed to me and thus empowers me to rejoice in the sufficiency of God's unmerited grace.

Each new day, I live in the knowledge and joy that Jesus has already healed me of the most deadly and destructive disease: sin. Moreover, Jesus has already given to me the gift of eternal life that comes through knowing Him. Jesus said: *I am the way, the truth and the life.'* My life is in Him, and He is my life.

Each new day, I wait to see whether God will heal me or take me. I have prayed all the prayers, laying down a deep foundation of supplication in which I entrust myself into the sovereignty of His will and purposes. Having done that, all I can do is wait upon the Lord to see what He will do.

Each new day, I live with the satisfying, comforting knowledge that in the end, cancer does not win; Jesus wins – always.

Each new day, I recognize that my greatest need is to know that I am at peace with God and made one with Him. Whether I live or whether I die, the ultimate goal is to be with the Lord: This is where faith in Jesus *always* works. Ultimately, this is where the death of a heating engineer, watersports instructor, ski guide, pastor, husband, father and believer is a required necessity for eternal life in Christ, for my identity and purpose is bound up in Him. As the Apostle Paul wrote:

'I have fought the good fight, I have finished the race, I have kept the faith' (2 Tim. 4:7).

'But we do not want you to be uninformed, brothers, about those who are asleep, that you may not grieve as others do who have no hope. For since we believe that Jesus died and rose again, even so, through Jesus, God will bring with him those who have fallen asleep. For this we declare to you by a word from the Lord, that we who are alive, who are left until the coming of the Lord, will not precede those who have fallen asleep. For the Lord himself will descend from heaven with a cry of command, with the voice of an archangel, and with the sound of the trumpet of God. And the dead in Christ will rise first. Then we who are alive, who are left, will be caught up together with them in the clouds to meet the Lord in the air, and so we will always be with the Lord. Therefore encourage one another with these words' (1 Thess. 4:13–18).

To God be the glory, great things He has done, is doing and will do.

JESUS MY DELIVERER

Jesus my deliverer
Name above all names
The glory of the universe
Your splendour forever remains.
You protect me in the path of your righteousness
King of kings you are my friend
You're my rock, my hope, my comforter
In you my praise shall find no end.

Your salvation from bondage rescues me
With joy my heart shall sing
For I will fear no evil one
Or the pain that sin may bring.
I trust in you my Saviour
You've paved for the way for me to come
Into your presence, love and majesty
The Kingdom of God's Son.

And so to you my conqueror
Saviour, Lord and King
To you I give my offering
To you my life I bring.
Onwards I will walk with you
As you lead me by your hand
Till at last my eyes shall see your face
In your Kingdom, gracious land
In your Kingdom, gracious land.

Amen

CPSIA information can be obtained
at www.ICGtesting.com
Printed in the USA
BVHW031005111021
618670BV00001B/6